CONTENTS

GETTING INTO

the Armed Forces

FIRST EDITION

FIONA HINDLE

TROTMAN

Getting into the Armed Forces
First edition

This first edition published in 2002
by Trotman and Company Ltd
2 The Green, Richmond, Surrey TW9 1PL

© Trotman and Company Limited 2002

British Library Cataloguing in Publication Data
A catalogue record for this book is available from the
British Library.

ISBN 0 85660 822 X

Typeset by Mac Style Ltd, Scarborough, N. Yorkshire

Printed and bound in Great Britain
by Bell & Bain Ltd

ABOUT THE AUTHOR

Fiona Hindle is an independent careers consultant, with a background in personnel. She has provided tailored careers consultancy to numerous businesses and organisations, we well as having written extensively on the legal profession, the City and the financial sector. Her clients include major companies as well as individuals of all ages considering career choice. Fiona was a careers adviser at the University of London Careers Service for many years and is experienced in the needs of graduate recruitment.

INTRODUCTION

The armed forces is made up of the Army, the Royal Air Force, the Royal Navy and the Royal Marines, and its primary purpose is to defend the interests of the UK at home and abroad.

The Army's role is to act as a fighting force on land. The Royal Air Force's role is to look after the UK's airspace. And the role of both the Royal Navy and Royal Marines is to act as a secure maritime defence force.

It is vital to the safety of the UK to have a strong and effective combined armed forces and, in order to do so, it recruits in the region of 20,000 young people annually. This book will tell you more about the entry requirements, the selection process, the personal qualities required, as well as the vast range of jobs and opportunities in each of the forces.

If you decide on life in the armed forces you will undoubtedly find that whether it is the Army, RAF, Navy or Marines that you join, they all offer far more than a job. Choosing to join the armed forces is choosing a way of life. And if you decide to join for only a few years rather than a lifelong career employers outside of the armed forces will value what you learn and many of the skills you gain.

THE COMMAND STRUCTURE

You will find that the Army, the RAF, the Royal Navy and the Royal Marines, each has its own traditions and methods of organisation. However, what they all have in common is a similar command structure, as follows:

Commissioned Officers

Commissioned officers are the leaders and managers across a wide range of technical and military functions and roles.

Non-commissioned Officers (NCOs)

These are the corporals, sergeants and warrant officers (or their equivalent in the Royal Navy and RAF). Their job is to take charge of smaller groups, and occasionally they may be called upon take up a specialist role, providing commissioned officers with technical guidance

Other personnel

These are soldiers in the Army, ratings in the Royal Navy and aircraftmen and aircraftwomen in the RAF. They may focus solely on military roles, or take the opportunity to learn the skills of a range of trades.

THE ARMY

Army officers and soldiers are engaged in assignments in over 30 countries around the world. The function of the Army is broad ranging, from looking after the security of the UK to issuing humanitarian relief to people in need.

The Army is organised into the Combat Arms, the Combat Support Arms and the Services, each with an essential role to play. Unlike the other services, you don't just 'join the Army' but have to make a decision right from the start to join a particular regiment or corps. Each has its own military function and, once you join, you will stay with that regiment or corps throughout your career.

THE ROYAL AIR FORCE

The RAF is structured into three commands: Strike Command, Logistics Command and Personnel and Training Command.

Strike Command is involved with flying and operating missile systems, plus having responsibility for units within the UK and abroad. The role of Logistics Command is to supply and maintain RAF operations all over the world. The purpose of Personnel and Training Command is to design, develop and deliver training courses to RAF personnel, as well as advising them on their career management.

Women are eligible to join all areas of the RAF other than the RAF Regiment. This is a specialist fighting force providing ground and short-range air defence anywhere in the world. Women are not able to join at present as it is thought they may not have the necessary physical strength to carry out all the required fighting duties.

THE ROYAL NAVY

Today, the role of the Royal Navy is to run a modern fleet of surface warships, ship-borne aircraft, as well as many support vessels. The fleet is supported at sea by the Navy's Submarine Service, which is well equipped with nuclear-powered and Trident submarines, in addition to a number of land-based communications centres, training establishments and other naval installations.

Surveying the world's oceans, the Navy also produces the world-famous Admiralty Charts, in addition to helping deal with any environmental disasters such as oil spills.

The Royal Navy is made up of six branches: Warfare, Engineering, Supply, Medical, Fleet Air Arm and the Submarine Service.

Men and women are trained and work alongside each other in all roles except on submarines and clearance diving.

THE ROYAL MARINES

The Royal Marines are the Navy's commandos, identified by their distinctive Green Beret, which they are awarded once they have passed the arduous and challenging demands of training. These men are highly trained and skilled in amphibious, jungle, mountain and arctic warfare.

3 Commando Brigade, as part of the Royal Marines Command, is the Royal Marines' principal operational formation, being a light amphibious infantry brigade with specialist mountain and extreme cold weather warfare expertise. The Brigade has considerable experience of operating with naval and air forces, from the UK and other countries that contribute forces to multi-national organisations such as UN and NATO.

The 3 Commando units: 40, 42 and 45 plus a range of supporting units are ultimately controlled by the Brigade Commander, based in Plymouth. They make up an integrated and self-sustaining force, capable of deploying as a single body or in smaller groups specifically designed to meet the needs of a particular task.

Occasionally the Commando Units serve in Northern Ireland and in recent years have also operated in Sierra Leone, Kosovo and The Congo.

Entry into the Royal Marines is open only to male entrants, except for the Royal Marines Band Service, where the positions of Musician and Bugler are open to both male and female entrants.

EQUAL OPPORTUNITIES

At present servicemen and women from ethnic minority groups make up just over 1 per cent of the armed forces. About 8 per cent of the total armed forces is made up of servicewomen. The armed forces continues to seek to expand career opportunities for women, but at the same time needs to make sure that they have the physical strength and capability to carry out all the required combat duties. Today, over 70 per cent of the posts in the Naval Service are open to women, around 70 per cent of posts in the Army and over 95 per cent of posts in the RAF. Women serve in combat roles both at sea and in the air, but some front-line posts, where sheer physical force and strength are necessary, are not open to women.

Please note that information can quickly change, so make sure you contact your Armed Forces Careers Office for current details.

LIFE IN THE ARMED FORCES

So, what's life really like in the armed forces today? Well, certainly there are opportunities that you'd be hard pressed to find in other jobs. But, at the same time, you need to be realistic. Think about your own standards and values and weigh up the pros and cons, as it is not necessarily a life that suits everyone.

You may have to face up to long separations from your family and friends. And, if you're in a combat role, you'll have to deal with some unique challenges and see some sights that you're not likely to encounter in any other job. And, at the early stages of your career, your earnings won't always be comparable to what you'd get in a job on 'Civvy Street'.

Many people in the armed forces describe it as an excellent lifestyle, full of adventure and excitement, with good job security and career progression. It is important that you do your research thoroughly, of course, but here's more of a flavour of what your life in the armed forces might be like.

CHALLENGE AND ADVENTURE

In today's armed forces you'll have the opportunity for an active life and to take part in some of the most adventurous activities you can imagine. Your way of life will change completely from the one you're used to. You'll be able to try sports you've never had the chance to try before, such as windsurfing, sailing, mountaineering, skiing, parachuting, scuba diving, horse-riding or even white-water rafting. And, within a short space of time, you'll be the fittest you've ever been. You'll meet new friends and have time for travel and adventure, often from the word 'go'.

If you're the sort of person who finds lots of changes stressful then perhaps it's not for you. In some jobs you'll be required to change both your job and location every two years. For some people this will be a benefit but for others ongoing change may be a less welcome challenge. But, investigate all opportunities, as there are many different types of jobs and you may just find your niche.

TEAMWORK AND MAKING NEW FRIENDS

In trying out these new experiences you'll gain confidence and belief in yourself, and through lots of team building exercises you'll build up trust in your teammates and learn how to get along with everyone. Effective teamwork and looking out for your teammates is the foundation of life in the armed forces. You'll get their support in return.

But, again, think hard about the sort of person you are. Are you at your best when you work in a team environment, or are you more suited to working independently? Life in the armed forces may be hard for someone who is more of a 'loner'.

SOCIAL LIFE

It's not all work – you'll have time to relax and have fun with your new mates, sharing experiences. The armed forces usually creates a very sociable community and you'll have the chance to take part in other activities such as a disco or a bowling night, or a fortnight's skiing in the Alps. The opportunities are there – if you want them.

You'll forge many good friendships and create a unique camaraderie with others who are all going through the same experience with you.

However, planning your holidays in advance can sometimes be a problem as you won't always know when you can take time off or where you'll be.

ACCOMMODATION, FACILITIES AND COMMUNAL LIVING

As far as accommodation is concerned, while you're training as a recruit or a junior officer you'll be required to live in accommodation on site.

But as soon as you take up your first post you'll be given housing appropriate to your rank.

You'll usually enjoy a range of facilities while you're there, including a cafeteria, bar and games room. And music provided by local bands or discos offers you entertainment most Saturday nights.

TRAINING

No matter how flexible you are, there's no doubt that when you start your training you'll be thrown into a new way of life. The training is intensive and all absorbing, giving you little time to think about anything else!

If at any time during the long and arduous training, it all gets a bit much for you there will be people who you can talk to who will be happy to help you and offer advice. It's not an easy journey for everyone; so don't be reluctant to ask for help.

DISCIPLINE AND TAKING ORDERS

Discipline, of course, is part of life in the armed forces, but it's there for the purpose of making sure everything runs fairly and smoothly. And this means making sure you wear your uniform in the correct way. If you're in the Navy, for example, once you're on a ship you'll soon see how limited the space is. Unless someone had ultimate responsibility for issuing orders, chaos would ensue.

After a few weeks you should get used to the discipline and understand why it's there. If you do have any difficulties your senior officers are there to help you. But, from the beginning, you'll need to be the kind of person who is motivated and self-disciplined and able to stand on your own two feet. A healthy dose of common sense is also invaluable.

BEING AWAY FROM HOME

And last, but not least, you need to ask yourself the questions: 'Am I prepared to live away from home, possibly in another country?' and 'Do

I like a challenge and am I willing to work in what can often be adverse conditions?'

The possible long spells away from home and resulting separation from friends and family can certainly be a hardship for some. So think carefully about the consequences and whether or not life in the armed forces is really for you.

THE ARMY

ENTRY REQUIREMENTS

Fitness

A high degree of physical fitness is important for all the armed forces. You'll need the following level of fitness to join the Army:

- able to run 1.5 miles in between 12 minutes 45 seconds and 14 minutes depending on your choice of job;
- able to do straight-arm heaves and abdominal curls to a reasonable standard;
- Pass a medical and live a drug free lifestyle.

Nationality

You must be a British citizen, a citizen of the Republic of Ireland or a Commonwealth citizen with unrestricted rights to live and work in the UK.

HOW CAN I JOIN AS A SOLDIER?

You will usually need to be between the ages of 16 and 30 when you join the Army as a soldier, and your parents must give their consent if you are under 18. Academic requirements are not always necessary, except for some technical jobs where you will require some GCSEs or equivalent in specific subjects. It is important that you contact your Armed Forces Careers Adviser for full information on current entry requirements.

What are my options in joining?

For most applicants your eligibility to join the Army, and your specific training route, will depend on the results you achieve on the Army

Entrance Test (known as BARB). BARB uses computer touch-screen question and answer techniques to find out your ability for training. See the section on Training.

Army Apprentices College

If you're aged between 16 and 18^1/$_2$ you can join the Army Apprentices College to study for an apprenticeship in one of the four Technical Corps. These are the Royal Engineers, the Royal Electrical and Mechanical Engineers, the Royal Corps of Signals and the Royal Logistic Corps. Contact your Armed Forces Careers Office for information on current available apprenticeships, which are usually available in the four Technical Corps and in the Royal Logistic Corps for Chefs and Marine Engineers.

As an Army apprentice you'll join the Army Apprentices College at Arborfield, where you'll spend eight months training, including the Apprentice Foundation Course learning basic military skills, study for relevant courses such as maths and engineering, as well as experiencing exercises and situations designed to develop your character and leadership skills. On completion of this part of your training you'll progress on to one of five national training centres for training in your specific trade, followed by on-the-job experience in an operational unit and subsequent further training at the appropriate national training centre to the required standard. On completion of your apprenticeship you should have reached NVQ Level 3 standard in your chosen specialism.

Army Foundation College

The Army Foundation College (AFC) is for those who wish to join the Infantry, the Royal Armoured Corps or the Royal Artillery. You must be aged between 16 and 17 years old to be eligible to go to the AFC to take the 42-week course, which includes all the basic military skills. This well-regarded course will give you the opportunity to improve your fitness level, teamwork, self-discipline and leadership skills through challenging activities such as abseiling, canoeing and climbing. You will also be able to gain qualifications in core skills, such as information technology, working with others and problem solving.

HOW CAN I JOIN AS AN OFFICER?

- Be over 17 years 9 months and under the age of 29 when you join.
- Have a minimum of five GCSEs (grades A–C, including English and Maths and a science subject or foreign language) plus two A-levels (grades A–E) or equivalent.
- It's not essential to have a degree, but over 85 per cent of Officer Cadets at Sandhurst are graduates.
- Some corps may require additional qualifications.
- Check with your Armed Forces Careers Adviser for full up-to-date details on entry requirements.

What will I be doing?

As an officer you will be a highly trained leader and manager so it's essential you're the sort of person who can cope with plenty of responsibility. Your initial training is designed to equip you with the appropriate skills to cope. Afterwards, you could have up to 30 men and women in your command and be responsible for their effectiveness, training and possibly even their lives. At times you'll have to work under extreme pressure, you'll work in many different countries, climates and conditions, and each job will give you more ability and experience.

What about when I'm not working?

The sporting facilities available to you as an Army officer are outstanding. You'll have plenty of time to develop and hone your skills in a vast range of sports, from mountaineering to sailing – even being encouraged to taking them to international level if you demonstrate good enough potential. And when you're not working or playing sport you will be able to enjoy relaxation time in the officers' mess, where there's always an abundance of social activities provided in friendly and comfortable surroundings.

If you decide to join the Army as an officer you'll have to give a lot and will find it demanding, but in return you'll have an enormous sense of achievement and will be very well looked after.

PERSONAL QUALITIES

What personal qualities will I need to join the Army?

- drive
- determination
- ability to handle responsibility
- able to work effectively as part of a team
- leadership potential
- ability to think quickly on your feet
- self-discipline
- self-confidence
- good level of physical fitness
- courage
- to be good at making decisions
- to have good communication skills
- numeracy
- focused
- trustworthy
- positive attitude.

The Army training is designed to bring these qualities out in you but you'll need to demonstrate that you have plenty of potential in the first place. All employers are likely to value such qualities but in the Army they are essential as it's highly possible there may be occasions when your actions affect the lives of others. In that situation you need to be able to think and react quickly. Your Army training will help you realise your potential and see just how much you can achieve when you have to. This will give you confidence and self-discipline that will stay with you for the rest of your life – whatever career path you take.

THE SELECTION PROCESS

All Candidates

Anyone who is interested in joining the Army has to pass a rigorous selection process, which includes aptitude tests, physical fitness assessments and interviews. This is to establish if you have the physical and mental potential for the job. The Army Entrance Test (BARB) is for those applying for soldier entry. If you're applying to be an officer you'll have different tests to sit. Regardless of whether or not you're applying to become a soldier or an officer you'll need to apply to join a particular regiment or corps. If you're unsure as to which to apply to, you'll be given advice from your Armed Forces Careers Adviser during the selection process.

OFFICER ENTRY

The role of an Army officer is both physically and intellectually demanding and their rigorous selection process is designed to ensure that you have all the qualities and potential to go on to become a successful officer.

The Interview

You will start the selection process with an interview to help you understand the wide range of opportunities open to you and help you begin to decide which part of the Army you wish to enter. This interview will often take place at school or university.

Corps or Regimental Sponsorship and Familiarisation

It is important to contact your Armed Forces Careers Office. Here, the Army Careers Adviser will guide you through the process and help you make contact with and visit a number of regiments and corps. This is necessary to help you decide which one you would be most suited to joining.

The Medical

All officer candidates have to go through a medical assessment. You don't have to be super-fit but you'll need to be in good shape both physically and mentally.

The Regular Commissions Board (RCB)

As an officer applicant, you'll attend the Regular Commissions Board. This is an intensive four-day selection designed to assess whether you have what it takes to be an officer in today's Army. There's a lot of information, such as 'Bringing out the leader in you', which will help you prepare for RCB. Contact your Armed Forces Careers Office for further details.

JOBS AND OPPORTUNITIES

The Army is made up of a series of regiments and corps with each one carrying out a particular military role and falling under one of three categories:

- Combat Arms
- Combat Support Arms
- Services.

COMBAT ARMS

The Combat Arms are the regiments and corps at the frontline of any battle and are specially trained to use the latest weapons and technology to overcome the enemy. They are also involved in the Army's peacekeeping activities worldwide.

The Household Cavalry provides armoured reconnaissance, using light tanks, as well as having a mounted regiment in London, performing ceremonial duties.

Jobs:

Tank Crewman/Mounted Dutyman

The Royal Armoured Corps spearheads attacks or strengthen defences, and also uses reconnaissance vehicles to gather information about the enemy's movements on the battlefield.

Jobs:

Tank Crewman – leading to crew specialisations as:

Driver
Gunner
Loader
Commander.

The Infantry is the largest part of the Army and uses a range of modern weapons and vehicles to get to the centre of the action.

Jobs:

Infantry Soldier (Guards, Scottish, Queen's, King's, Prince of Wales's and Light Divisions, Parachute and Royal Irish Regiments) leading to specialisations as:

Sniper
Mortarman
Anti-Tank Missileman
Reconnaissance Patrolman
Machine Gunner
Assault Pioneer
Communications & Data Processor
Medical Orderly
Regimental Policeman
Drummer, Piper or Bugler
Driver.

Special Air Service Regiment (SAS)

Contact your Armed Forces Careers office for further information.

The Army Air Corps attacks enemy armour, provides additional reconnaissance and transports men and stores to and from the battlefield.

Jobs:

Groundcrew incorporating:

> Driver
> Signaller
> Fuel Bowser Operator
> and leading to Air Crew/Pilot (Corporals and above).

COMBAT SUPPORT ARMS

Fighting in close support of the Combat Arms, the Combat Support Arms provide artillery, field engineering, signals and intelligence back up.

The Royal Regiment of Artillery delivers the heavy bombardment that precedes any attack using sophisticated artillery and missile systems.

Jobs:

Crewman – specialising as:

> Gunner Field Guns
> Gunner Multiple Launch Rocket System (MLRS)
> Gunner Driver
> Storeman Technical

Crewman Technical – specialising as:

> Gunner Surface to Air Missile
> Signaller
> Command Post Assistant Guns/Air Defence/MLRS/Phoenix
> Meteorological Assistant
> Special Observer
> Surveyor
> Surveyor Sound Ranging
> Observation Post-Assistant
> Radar Operator Field
> Naval Gunfire Assistant

Mounted Gunner – specialising as:

> Mounted Gunner
> Farrier
> Saddler
> Tailor.

The Corps of Royal Engineers build and demolish bridges, roads and airfields, construct camps, fuel installations and port facilities, and lays and clear minefields.

Jobs:

Military Engineer A – specialising as:

> Heating & Plumbing
> Electrician
> Plant Operator Mechanic
> Fitter General

Military Engineer B – specialising as:

> Bricklayer & Concretor
> Building & Structural Finisher
> Carpenter & Joiner
> Fabricator

Military Engineer (C3 Systems)
Military Engineer (Driver)
Military Engineer (Design) – specialising as:

> Construction Materials Technician
> Surveying Engineering
> Design Draughtsman
> Draughtsman Electrical & Mechanical

Military Engineer (Geo Tech) – specialising as:

> Terrain Analysis
> Reprography
> Topography.

The Royal Corps of Signals provides the Army with modern telecommunications and information systems

Jobs:

Communications Logistics Group – specialising as:

> Royal Signals Driver
> Technical Supply Specialist

Electronic Warfare Group – specialising as:

> Specialist Operator
> Linguist Operator

Technician Group – specialising as:

> Systems Engineering Technician
> Installation Technician

Operator Group – specialising as:

> Radio Systems Operator
> Area Systems Operator

Electrician Group – specialising as:

> Royal Signals Electrician

The Intelligence Corps collects and analyses information about the enemy and provides security intelligence to combat espionage, subversion and terrorism.

Jobs:

Operator Intelligence and Security
Operator Special Intelligence (Linguist)
Operator Special Intelligence (Analyst).

SERVICES

The corps and regiments of the Services provide vital technical, logistical and administrative support to the Combat Arms and the Combat Support Arms.

The Royal Logistics Corps provides and distributes the Army's food, supplies and equipment and transports personnel and freight by land, sea and air.

Jobs:

Pioneer
Driver
Driver Radio Operator
Air Despatcher
Port Operator
Movement Controller
Seaman/Seawoman
Postal and Courier Operator
Petroleum Operator
Supply Controller
Supply Specialist
Ammunition Technician
Chef.

The Corps of Royal Electrical and Mechanical Engineers maintains and repairs the Army's vehicles, arms and weapons systems on base and in the field.

Jobs:

Vehicle Mechanic
Vehicle Electrician
Metalsmith
Armourer
Gunfitter
Electronics Technician
Telecommunications Technician
Radar Technician
Avionics Technician
Aircraft Technician
Storeman/Storewoman
Recovery Mechanic
Regimental Specialist

The Adjutant General's Corps provides the Army's personnel and legal services, education and training, as well as the Military Police.

Jobs:

Military Clerk
Policeman/Policewoman.

Army Medical Services are responsible for the medical and dental care of all the Army's men, women and animals at home and in the field. They consist of: The Royal Army Medical Corps, the Royal Army Dental Corps, Queen Alexandra's Royal Army Nursing Corps and the Royal Army Veterinary Corps.

Jobs:

Royal Army Medical Corps

    Combat Medical Technician
    Environment Health Technician
    Operating Health Technician
    Pharmacy Technician
    Radiographer

Royal Army Dental Corps

    Dental Support Specialist
    Dental Technician
    Dental Hygienist

Queen Alexandra's Royal Army Nursing Corps

    Registered General Nurse
    Registered Nurse (Mental Health)
    Student Nurse General
    Healthcare Assistant

Royal Army Veterinary Corps

    Dog Trainer
    Trainee Farrier
    Veterinary Technician.

The Royal Army Chaplains' Department.

Jobs:

Chaplain.

Corps of Army Music, which includes 30 bands of professional musicians

Jobs:

Musician.

TRAINING

TRAINING AS A SOLDIER

Basic Training

Basic training for all single entry soldiers lasts between 12 and 22 weeks. As a new recruit you'll join one of five Army Training Regiments and will spend between 1 and 11 weeks on the Army Foundation Scheme. The exact number of weeks you'll be there will dependant on your aptitude and fitness. This part of Army training is all about helping you to adapt to Army life, as well as bringing your stamina and fitness to the required level. Afterwards you'll spend another 11 weeks training under the Common Military Syllabus, which is a mixture of classroom and practical instruction in a range of subjects from map reading to defensive measures in nuclear, biological and chemical warfare. This part of the training will further increase your motivation, working with others in a team and your physical fitness. If you pass this stage of the training you'll be awarded an NVQ/SVQ Level 1 in Public Services, before leaving the ATR and joining your arm or service for specific training in your chosen job.

Army apprenticeship

The Army can train you in over 100 trades. Army apprenticeships are usually available in one of the four technical corps: the Royal Engineers; the Royal Corps of Signals; the Royal Logistic Corps (Chefs and Marine Engineers); the Royal Electrical and Mechanical Engineers.

The Army Apprentices College is based at Arborfield and you'll spend your first eight months following the Apprentice Foundation Course, including the 11-week Common Military Syllabus. During this time you'll study maths, science, engineering, material drawing, communications and IT. But considerable importance is also given to your own personal development, leadership training and social education.

Further training in the specific trade you've chosen, plus some practical experience in an operational unit, follows this. All students should expect to complete their apprenticeship with at least an NVQ level 3 in their chosen trade.

Army Foundation College

If you wish to join the Infantry, the Royal Armoured Corps or the Royal Artillery you'll have to apply to and attend the Army Foundation College (AFC). Women are not allowed to join the Royal Armoured Corps and Infantry, but the Royal Artillery is open to both men and women. Candidates for the AFC can apply to Armed Forces Careers Offices from the age of 15. Based in Harrogate, the AFC will put you through 42-week course of skills training to improve your physical fitness and self-discipline, develop some basic military skills, and increase your leadership ability through a range challenging activities, such as abseiling, canoeing and climbing.

When you join the Army as a soldier you will be a Private. After a series of training courses and promotions you'll be able to progress through the ranks and, if you are recommended, you can go on to be commissioned as an officer. Along the way, the Army can help you to gain GCSEs, A-levels and even a degree.

TRAINING AS AN OFFICER

The training you'll receive as an Army officer is recognised throughout the world, which will also allow you to go on to qualify in a wide range of specialisms.

Sandhurst

Army Officers undergo their training at the Royal Military Academy Sandhurst (RMAS). This is where you'll learn the leadership skills necessary to manage a team of trained soldiers, inspiring their confidence, trust and respect.

You'll spend 11 months attending the commissioning course at Sandhurst. It's an exceptionally demanding course designed to challenge you physically, mentally and emotionally. You'll learn the essentials you need in the Army, such as survival skills, but most importantly you'll also be trained in finding out how to get the most out of yourself, your soldiers and your equipment. You will often be pushed to the limit but come out the stronger for it. In going through such training you'll bond with your fellow officers and will build many friendships that will last a lifetime.

The Royal Military Academy Sandhurst has three annual intakes – January, May and September.

After completing your training at Sandhurst you'll join your regiment or corps and train for your specialist role as a platoon or troop commander. Training continues and there will be numerous opportunities to take more qualifications and even the possibility of professional examinations.

The Army Commission

Many people look for a long-term career as an Army officer, while others choose to stay for a shorter period and then take their experience and training into a civilian career. The Army offers a range of commissions designed to suit your needs.

Short Service Commission (SSC)

An SSC is the normal first commission for those who wish to be an officer in the Army. SSCs offer a career lasting a minimum of three years (six years in the Army Air Corps) and a maximum of eight years from leaving Sandhurst. After two years an SSC officer can apply to convert to an Intermediate Regular Commission, upon a recommendation.

Intermediate Regular Commission (IRC)

An IRC offers you a mid-length career and entitles you to serve for a maximum of 16 years, entitling you to an immediate Army pension. Alternatively, after two years you may apply for one of the following:

Regular Commission (RC)

A RC offers a full career, potentially to the age of 55. It is awarded to Undergraduate Cadets and recommended IRC officers who have had a minimum two years' IRC service.

Gap Year Commission (GYC)

This is the ideal chance to discover the lifestyle and challenge of an officer role without any commitment to a career. A GYC is open to anyone aged between 18 and 20 with a definite place at a UK university for a first degree. It can last anything between 4 and 18 months and applicants need to be recommended by their head-teacher, be unmarried, pass an Army Medical Board and pass the Regular Commissions Board with a special recommendation for GYC.

Financial Sponsorship

The Army offers a range of financial sponsorship schemes to help you start your Army career, in addition to gaining some support to finish your education. Here are some of them, but contact your Armed Forces Careers Office for full, up-to-date information on current schemes available.

Army Scholarships

These offer financial support for your parents or guardians for your A-level education, followed by sponsorship for you at university and a lump sum on entering Sandhurst. If you're successful you'll offered a Short Service Commission.

Welbeck Sixth-Form College

This is the Army's prestigious sixth form college, which offer a science-based A-level syllabus to men and women interested in joining one of the Army's Technical or Engineering Corps. If successful, the College will guarantee you a degree course paid as an Officer Cadet at the Royal Military College of Science followed by a place at Sandhurst.

The Army Undergraduate Bursary

This offers a tax-free grant for up to four years at university followed by a lump sum payment on entering Sandhurst, leading to a Short Service Commission.

Army Medical Cadetship
This offers sponsorship for students studying to become doctors, dentists or vets.

CAREER PATHS

Career Development for Soldiers

Having first joined the Army as a Private, after completing various promotion courses and trade tests you'll have the chance to progress through the rank structure from Lance Corporal to Corporal, then to Sergeant and to Warrant Officer. If you're recommended, and gain the relevant qualifications, you'll be given the opportunity of being commissioned as an officer.

Career Development for Officers

The first of the officer ranks is Second Lieutenant and this is where you'll start your career. After a couple of years will likely be promoted to Lieutenant. In a further two or three years, all going well, you'll receive a promotion to Captain, and then Major.

SALARIES

Young soldiers (under 17½)	£8,001 pa
Adults	
Private over 17½) on entry	£10,344 pa
Private Level 1	£12,071 pa
Private Level 3	£13,490 pa
Private Level 4	£14,673 pa
Lance Corporal	£16,801 pa
Corporal	£19,812 pa
Sergeant	£22,926 pa
Staff Sergeant	£25,298 pa
Warrant Officer Class II	£27,532 pa
Warrant Officer Class I	£29,182 pa

The above rates show the most common basic pay rates and do not include length of service increments.

Contact your Armed Forces Careers Office for current rates of pay.

Additional pay

Certain specialists (eg parachutists) receive additional pay and those permanently stationed in Northern Ireland receive a resident supplement. Additional benefits include a local overseas allowance payable to offset the extra costs of living overseas.

Pensions

All soldiers receiving full time pay are members of the non-contributory armed forces Pension Scheme. Soldiers are eligible for an immediate pension and lump sum after completing 22 years' service from the age of 18.

PROFILES

CASE STUDY

Officer Chloe Brown

A former pupil of Nonsuch Grammar School in Cheam, Chloe Brown always knew she wanted a job in the education arena; however, unlike most she also decided she wanted her teaching career to take off within the Army.

Having been a cadet at school, Chloe already had some idea of what Army life entailed, and was awarded an Army sponsorship at the age of 15 that took her through school and university (neatly avoiding the money worries of many other young students!)

Chloe then spent 11 months at Sandhurst – the Royal Military Academy where students train to become officers. During this time she was trained in skills that are now proving invaluable in her teaching field, such as teamwork, organisational, time management and leadership skills.

'*I love travel and foreign cultures,*' Chloe explains. '*I took my degree in French, Russian and European Studies and was keen for more! A career in the Army offers me so many opportunities.*' Unlike that of a civilian teacher's, Chloe's job takes her all over the world. In the coming year she is taking part in an operational tour in Kosovo, followed by an expedition in Nepal, but Chloe knows that these plans could change at any time and it is that variety and challenge that makes her passionate about her job.

Chloe also has another reason for loving Army life, as it was here that she met her partner who she recently married!

Chloe offers her advice to youngsters still at school and interested in an Army career: *'If you are interested, at least try to pass selection − it could open new doors for you and the opportunities are endless. The familiarisation visits are also a great way to find out what the Army has to offer.'*

Private Leroy Smith, aged 20

Leroy has benefited not just from the opportunity to gain qualifications in the Army but also the chance to develop personal skills such as discipline and self-motivation, all with a guaranteed pay cheque at the end of the month!

Leroy has had experiences in the Army that would daunt most young people leaving home for the first time. His most challenging time was a three-week jungle-training course learning survival skills in Kenya. His most significant achievement was giving vital medical assistance to an injured soldier in Kosovo.

Gunner Dave Southall, aged 20

Dave worked for three years as a lift engineer in the City. He'd often considered a career in the Army, having been a cadet at school in Dagenham, but he also wanted to pursue his passion for music. He taught himself the trumpet as a youngster but did not have any formal music qualifications. He had visited the King's Troop many times to see his friend who was Trumpet Major, who persuaded him to join. His biggest challenge was learning to ride as he had never even sat on a horse before! Dave now plays as one of the Troop's trumpeters on parade and his proudest moment was playing in a fanfare in front of Her Majesty The Queen at the Royal Tournament. As a lift engineer he was working behind the scenes, but now that he is in the public eye, his mother is particularly proud as her friends are always calling to say they've seen her son on the TV! *'Being in the Army is absolutely superb,'* says Dave. *'There aren't many jobs on "civvy street" that offer you the chance to travel the world, and have a guaranteed pay cheque at the end of the month!'*

THE ROYAL AIR FORCE

ENTRY REQUIREMENTS

AIRMEN/AIRWOMEN

You'll need to be between the ages of 16 and 29 for most roles in the RAF. There are over 70 jobs in total, including some that require no formal qualifications. However, there are a number of exceptions, and entry qualifications vary depending upon the trade you wish to pursue, so it's important to contact your nearest Armed Forces Careers Office for full and up-to-date information.

OFFICERS

Branch	Age on entry	Minimum qualifications
Pilot	Under 24	5 GCSEs + 2 A-levels (or equivalent)
Weapons Systems Officer	Under 26	5 GCSEs + 2 A-levels (or equivalent)
Air Traffic Control	Under 30	5 GCSEs + 2 A-levels (or equivalent)
Fighter Control	Under 30	5 GCSEs + 2 A-levels (or equivalent)
Intelligence	Under 30	5 GCSEs + 2 A-levels (or equivalent)
Flight Operations	Under 30	5 GCSEs + 2 A-levels (or equivalent)
RAF Regiment	Under 26	5 GCSEs + 2 A-levels (or equivalent)
Provost/Security	Under 30	5 GCSEs + 2 A-levels (or equivalent)
Supply	Under 30	5 GCSEs + 2 A-levels (or equivalent)
Administration	Under 35	5 GCSEs + 2 A-levels (or equivalent)
Medical Support	Under 35	5 GCSEs + 2 A-levels (or equivalent)
Training	Under 39	Degree
Catering	Under 39	Degree
Engineer	Under39	Degree

Physical Education	Under27	Degree
Medical	Under 55	Professional
Dental	Under 55	Professional
Nursing	23–38	Professional
Chaplain	26–39	Professional
Legal	Under 30	Professional

NCO AIRCREW

(See page 2 of the 'Introduction' for explanation of NCO)

Branch	Age on entry	Minimum qualifications
Weapons Systems Operator	Under 31	5 GCSEs (Grade C) or equivalent
Air Loadmaster	Under 31	5 GCSEs (Grade C) or equivalent

It is important to note that there are also height, weight and size restrictions, which could affect your application. You will also have to be physically fit with a body mass in proportion with your height. Contact your Armed Forces Careers Office for up-to-date details.

PERSONAL QUALITIES

Similar to all the armed forces, if you join the RAF it is vitally important that you get along with other people. You'll often be working and living closely as part of a team and you must be able to:

- take orders
- react immediately to a situation
- give and take and demonstrate flexibility
- work well with other people.

Being in the services is a lot more than just a job – it's a way of life, which you'll live and breathe.

THE SELECTION PROCESS

Stage 1

After your initial enquiry, and on the basis that you're eligible, you'll be given an application for service in the RAF and invited to attend the Armed Forces Careers Office (AFCO) for an aptitude test, medical and interview.

Stage 2

There are three parts to Stage 2 and to be successful you must pass all three parts.

Part 1 – Aptitude and ability tests

This involves sitting seven tests lasting about 90 minutes at your nearest AFCO. The tests are designed specifically to assess your verbal, numerical and reasoning ability, short-term memory, ability to perform tasks quickly and accurately, and understanding of basic electrical and mechanical principles. Not all of the test scores will be considered for selection to every trade. All the tests are multiple choice and are timed. If you fail the aptitude tests you are allowed another attempt after six months has elapsed.

You will be given the results of the aptitude tests by a member of the AFCO staff, who will also advise you on which trades you're eligible for and their current availability.

Part 2 – Medical

If you've passed the aptitude tests and there are vacancies for your chosen trade(s), the next part is to take a hearing and medical examination. The level of medical fitness required for the RAF is high and it's not uncommon for some people to have more than one medical examination.

Part 3 – Selection interview

An RAF corporal or sergeant will conduct a formal interview, lasting from 30–45 minutes, asking you about your family background, education, any previous jobs, interests, what sports you play and what you know about the RAF. The purpose of this interview is for the RAF to find out more about you and for you to find out more about the RAF. A second selection interview may follow with a commissioned officer, flight sergeant or sergeant.

If you are successful in all three parts at Stage 2 you can go on to Stage 3 or 4, depending on the trades you have applied for.

Stage 3

Some trades require you to pass additional specialist tests and interviews, designed to assess aptitudes and skills specific to your chosen trade. At this stage you might be invited to an RAF station.

Stage 4

If you've been successful so far you'll be considered for a vacancy in your chosen trade(s).

Stage 5

This stage will require you to attend a further interview for a formal Offer of Service about eight weeks before you join the RAF. This is usually a formal interview with a commissioned officer or a flight sergeant.

Selection for aircrew and to train as an officer takes place at the Officers and Aircrew Selection Centre (OASC) at the RAF College Cranwell. Here potential pilots, navigators and non-commissioned aircrew spend four days taking a challenging series of aptitude tests, exercises, a medical and interviews. If you don't make the grade for flying duties you will be counselled and may be considered for other duties.

JOBS AND OPPORTUNITIES

The RAF is organised into three commands:

- Strike Command
- Logistics Command
- Personnel and Training Command.

Strike Command is directly concerned with flying and operating missile systems.

Logistics Command supplies and maintains RAF operations worldwide.

Personnel and Training Command designs, develops and delivers training programmes to RAF personnel looking after their training and career progression.

The jobs listed below are found in all three commands.

Support Trades – Airwatch

Flight Operations Assistants
Personnel Administrators
Flight Operations Assistants (Air Traffic Controller)
Aerospace Systems Operators

Support Trades – Secretarial and Administration

Physical Training Instructors
Musicians

Support Trades – Security

Firefighters
RAF Police
RAF Regiment Gunners

Support Trades – Catering

Chefs
Catering Accountants
Stewards

Medical and Dental

Dental Hygienists
Dental Technicians
Dental Nurses
Radiographers
Operating Theatre Technicians
Staff Nurses (RGN)
Laboratory Technicians

Medical Assistants
Pharmacy Technicians
Student Nurses
Staff Nurses (RMN)
Environmental Health Technicians

Support Trades – Supply and Movements

Suppliers
Movement Operators
Mechanical Transport Drivers

Support Trades – Safety and Surface

Painters and Finishers
Survival Equipment Fitters

Support Trades – Telecommunications

Telecommunications Operators
Intelligence Analysts (Voice)
Intelligence Analysts (Communications)
Aerial Erectors

Support Trades – Photography

Photographers
Intelligence Analysts (Imagery)
Air Cartographers

Support Trades – Engineering

Technician Apprenticeships are available for all engineering trades and every Technician Apprentice is enrolled for a Level 3 NVQ. Every year there may be a limited number of places available for those who fail to meet the minimum academic requirements for Apprenticeship but who, nevertheless, perform particularly well in the RAF aptitude tests and possess suitable personal qualities.

Aircraft Engineers
Mechanical Transport Technicians
Airframe Technicians
Ground Electronics Technicians

Aircraft Electrical Technicians
Avionics Technicians
Propulsion Technicians
General Technicians (Ground Support Equipment)
General Technicians (Workshops)
General Technicians (Electrical)
Weapons Technicians

Officers

Pilots
Air Traffic Controllers
Fighter Controllers
Aerosystems
Communications/Electronics
Flight Operations Officers
Navigators
Intelligence Officers
The RAF Regiment
Supply Officers
Training Officers
Administrative/Secretarial Officers
Catering Officers
Dental Officers
Physical Education Officers
Provost Officers
Nursing Officers
Medical Officers
Chaplains
Legal Officers

Non-commissioned Aircrew

If your ambition is to be part of the RAF's flying team there are three non-commissioned RAF Aircrew roles that offer you the opportunity to become an advanced specialist on flying duties.

Air Electronics Operators
Air Electronics Operators can be flying on marine patrol in a Nimrod, locating, identifying and tracking surface craft and submarines.

Air Loadmaster
Air Loadmasters work in a wide range of fixed-wing aircraft and helicopters, making performance calculations and ensuring passengers or cargo are loaded, carried and unloaded quickly and safely.

Air Signallers
Air Signallers primarily system operators monitoring and manipulating specialised, complex electronic reconnaissance equipment.

TRAINING

TRAINING AS AN AIRMAN AND AIRWOMAN

You will spend your first seven weeks on the Recruit Training Course at RAF Halton or RAF Honington (RAF Regiment only). This stage of your training is designed to get you physically fit and build up your stamina.

Next comes your trade training, lasting anything from three weeks to three years depending on the trade you choose. Once you've completed your training successfully you'll be posted to an RAF establishment, either in this country or overseas, and begin working under supervision.

If you're keen to progress and you pass promotion and trade-training tests, you'll be able to advance through the rank structure from Leading Aircraftman/Aircraftwoman to Senior Aircraftman/Aircraftwoman, then to Corporal, on to Sergeant, from there to Chief Technician (in some trades only) and then to Flight Sergeant and finally to Warrant Officer. At any time, if you gain the required qualifications, you can apply to become an officer.

OFFICER TRAINING

The first step to gaining your commission is to complete the 24-week Initial Officer Training (IOT) course, designed to fully develop your leadership skills. If you've been selected for a specialist branch to which you bring additional professional skills you'll undertake the 8-week

Specialist Entry and Re-entry course. This applies to Medical, Dental, Nursing and Legal Officers and to RAF Chaplains.

Your Initial Officer Training starts with getting you into a military mode of thinking and acting. You will also undergo considerable leadership training, ending with a field leadership camp. You'll spend some time in the classroom learning how the RAF works, including Air Force Law and how to look after those in your charge. Finally, you'll undertake an intensive, practical exercise to demonstrate you have mastered all the skills you've learnt. And if successful, you'll graduate as an RAF officer.

A high level of physical fitness is very important for Initial Officer Training so it's to your advantage to get into good shape before you start. A number of weeks before commencing your course you'll be invited to the RAF College Cranwell for a familiarisation visit. At this time you'll be asked to complete part of the RAF Fitness Test, which consists of an aerobic test. If you fail the test you'll be given advice and the opportunity to take it again when you arrive at the RAF College to begin IOT. But it's essential that you do pass the fitness test, otherwise you won't be able to start your training.

When you undertake your IOT course you'll have the rank of officer cadet or student officer and will usually graduate as a flying officer or pilot officer. When you've completed your professional training you'll probably spend up to two years in one post on your first tour before moving on to a second posting, aimed to expand your experience as much as possible within your specialisation. Your responsibilities will continue to grow as you progress and develop within your branch or branch specialisation, and as you gain more and more experience you'll find that most officers have the opportunity for a staff job in one of the RAF command centres. If you want to go for promotion above the rank of flight lieutenant, in the majority of branches you'll need to compete for however many vacancies are available within your branch at the time.

Once you've graduated from the Initial Officer Training course you are starting your career with the RAF, which will give you ongoing training. You'll receive continuous training, no matter which branch you join, during the entire period of your commission. It may also be possible for you to gain further professional qualifications, sponsored by the RAF, as well as gaining exceptional management experience.

CAREER PATHS

If you are ambitious and have the appropriate skills, personal qualities and motivation, no matter at what level you join the RAF it is possible to take your career right to the very top of the ladder.

Engagement

A regular engagement for nine years is the norm if you join in any of the support trades. After this it may be possible to re-engage so that you can complete 22 years' service. This would then qualify you for a pension, or, if you wished, to stay in the RAF until you're 55 years of age.

There is some flexibility if you're under the age of 17 years 6 months when you enlist – you'll be able to leave on a free discharge during your first six months of service if you wish. However, this only applies after you've completed at least 28 days of your training. It is also possible to give notice after you've completed three years' service after your training.

You will be given plenty of opportunity to gain academic qualifications through private study, supported by the RAF, which helps many aircraftmen and aircraftwomen to progress in their career to NCO aircrew training or apply for a commission.

Commissions

There are two types of commission open to you.

Permanent Commission (PC)
On a Permanent Commission you will serve as an officer to the age of 38 or until you have completed 16 years from the age of 21, whichever is the longer. For those who wish it is possible to serve beyond this date until the age of 55, after which you'll be entitled to a generous pension and gratuity.

Short Service Commission (SSC)
The length of a Short Service Commission depends on your branch.

As a pilot or navigator you'll be offered a 12-year commission, whereas the majority of ground-based specialisations are offered for six years.

This will enable officers to complete training and a minimum of two tours of duty. However, there are some exceptions, including direct entrant Medical Officers and Dental Officers, who can be offered three-year commissions, and Nursing Officers and Chaplains, who are usually offered four-year commissions.

NCO aircrew entry

As NCO aircrew you'll initially enlist for 12 years. But you'll have the option of signing on again for a total of 22 years' service or until you retire at the age of 55. It is common for NCO aircrew to apply for a commission and progress to become an officer in their particular specialisation.

Rank structure

The RAF has two rank structures – one for commissioned officers and one for the other ranks.

Commissioned ranks

Pilot Officer
Flying Officer
Flight Lieutenant
Squadron Leader
Wing Commander
Group Captain
Air Commodore
Air Vice-Marshal
Air Marshal
Air Chief Marshal
Marshal of the Royal Air Force

Other ranks

Leading Aircraftman/Aircraftwoman
Senior Aircraftman/Aircraftwoman
Junior Technician (Technical trades only)
Corporal
Sergeant

Chief Technician (Technical trades only)
Flight Sergeant
Warrant Officer/Master Aircrew

SALARIES

RAF rates of pay are reviewed every year by the Armed Forces Pay
Review Body and are based on a comprehensive military salary structure
designed to be comparable with civilian salaries for similar jobs. For
current rates of pay contact your Armed Forces Careers Office.

Pay on entry and during recruit training

Rank	Per annum
Aircraftman/woman	£10,344
Leading Aircraftman/woman	£12,070
Senior Aircraftman/woman	Minimum £12,782 up to £22,100
Junior Technician	Minimum £15,461 up to £22,100

Pay on promotion to Corporal and above

Rank	Per annum
Corporal	£19,812 up to £25,341
Sergeant	£22,925 up to £28,199
Chief Technician	£25,298 up to £32,109
Flight Sergeant	£25,298 up to £33,028
Warrant Officer	£29,181 up to £35,420

Basic pay

Officers of the General Duties, Operations Support, Engineer, Supply,
Administrative, Medical Support and Legal branches, and officers of the
Princess Mary's Royal Airforce Nursing Service (PMRAFNS), receive
the following rates of basic pay:

Rank	Per annum
Officer Cadet	£11,888
Acting Pilot Officer	£16,654
Pilot Officer	£18,797
Flying Officer	£22,597 up to maximum of £24,973
Flight Lieutenant	£28,813 up to £34,269
Squadron Leader	£36,295 up to £43,471
Wing Commander	£51,191 up to £56,585

PROFILE

CASE STUDY

Jonathan Irvine – University Air Squadron

Officer Cadet Jonathan Irvine is 21 years of age and in the process of finishing his final year of a biochemistry degree at university. He joined the UAS in his second year.

'Without any commitment, joining the UAS has given me the chance to find out so much more about the RAF and help me decide if it's the career for me. It's been an ideal opportunity for me and I've gained some fantastic experience. I was lucky and passed the selection process first time, including the preliminary interview, the medical and then the in-depth interview. I was really keen to join and I think that was important in coming across at the interviews.

'Initially when I joined the UAS my first experience of flying was at the special induction weekend. We all went on a familiarisation flight and were given the appropriate flying kit to wear. There's a huge amount to learn, especially at the beginning as you're starting from nothing, but it does begin to get easier as you keep pace with your study guide and host of other manuals. For everyone, their first flight is unforgettable and gives you such a sense of achievement – I feel it's opened up a whole new world to me!'

THE ROYAL NAVY

In the Royal Navy every day brings new challenges and people with a vast range of different skills are required – from computer operators and engineers to medical assistants and cooks.

ENTRY REQUIREMENTS

JOINING AS A RATING

With your parents' consent you can join the Royal Navy at the age of 16 and serve for as little as four years from your 18th birthday. But if you decide in the early stages that the Navy isn't your future then it's possible for you to leave.

When you join you'll meet many other people of your age, often resulting in some lifelong friendships. There are many jobs in the Navy that don't require you to have qualifications, but if you have some GCSEs then you'll have more opportunities and the Navy will train you in the specific skills you need.

OPEN ENGAGEMENT

As a Royal Navy recruit you'll join on an 'Open Engagement'. This means you're committed to stay in the Navy for at least four years after you finish your training, or from your 18th birthday. But if you decide in the first three months that the Navy is not for you then you can leave.

However, if you decide to stay, you'll be offered 22 years' paid and pensionable employment. If you change your mind you can leave any time after the age of 20 years and 6 months by giving 18 months' notice (this may vary according to the length of your training for some of the skilled branches). So there is an escape route if you decide the Navy is not for you.

JOINING AS AN OFFICER

If you join the Royal Navy as an officer you'll be given a lot of responsibility, both for other people but also for state-of-the-art equipment, which could be anything from commanding a warship in the Atlantic to flying a Lynx helicopter. And as a Naval Officer you'll receive specialist training to equip you to carry out key operational roles.

Officer specialisms include Warfare, Aviation, Diving, Royal Marines, Hydrographic and Meteorology, Engineering, Supply and Training Management. In addition there are also Medical and Dental Officers, Queen Alexandra's Royal Navy Nursing Service (QARNNS) and Chaplains, all playing their own role in the Royal Navy.

So what do you need to join the Navy as an officer?

A-levels (or equivalent)
Well, if you're studying for A-levels or equivalent, you could join as an Officer directly, starting as a Midshipman and progressing to Sub-Lieutenant after two years. And if you're taking maths and science subjects you could apply for an engineering degree at the University of Southampton under the Engineering Sponsorship Scheme.

Graduate or professional qualifications
If you're a graduate or have professional qualifications you can join the Navy as a Sub-Lieutenant. By the time you reach your early 30s you'll probably have progressed to the middle-management grade of Lieutenant Commander.

University sponsorship (see page 74 for further details)
The Navy may be able to offer you sponsorship if you're applying to university. Bursaries are paid over and above a Local Education Authority (LEA) grant and you remain a civilian while you study. If you're very able and want to become an officer in one of the following branches – Warfare, Supply, Engineer or Aircrew – you may be entitled to a university cadetship.

But no matter at which point you enter the Royal Navy you'll receive training in your own specialist area, plus the opportunity for further education as part of your initial training. Along the way you'll also be trained in the necessary management skills to help you succeed in your career.

PERSONAL QUALITIES

What personal qualities will I need to join the Royal Navy?

There are as many different types of people in the Navy as there are jobs. However everyone, regardless of rank, has two things in common:

- the willingness to work hard
- the ability to adapt to new situations by learning.

THE SELECTION PROCESS

Once you've applied the staff at the Armed Forces Careers Office will help and advise you to make the best career choice. They'll ask you to decide if you want to join the Royal Navy, the Royal Marines or Queen Alexandra's Royal Navy Nursing Service. And within these three Services you'll be asked to choose a particular job, called a 'Branch of Choice'. But, although you may receive guidance from your Careers Adviser, the ultimate choice between the three Services, and then the Branch of Choice in your chosen Service, has to be your own.

It is important to note that once you've entered there's no allowance for you to change your mind and transfer to a different Branch of Choice. So it is essential that you're perfectly sure about your Branch of Choice before you enter. Once you've made your decision you will go through the following stages.

Stage 1

Along with the other candidates you will gather at the Armed Forces Careers Office, where you'll start the selection procedure by completing a five-part questionnaire, which includes information on:

- Family details
- School and education
- Work
- Hobbies and pastimes
- Why you want to join the RN/RM/QARNNS.

After completing this you'll be asked to sit an academic test, consisting of four parts; containing multiple choice questions on reasoning, English language, numeracy and mechanical comprehension.

Stage 2 (Artificer Apprentices only)

If you're applying to be an Artificer Apprentice (see Warfare Branch, page 46), once you've successfully completed Stage 1, you'll be required to take a further test of 40 mental arithmetic questions (of minimum GCSE grade 'C' standard).

Stage 3

This stage consists of an interview lasting about 30-40 minutes. A Naval Careers Adviser will conduct it. This interview is your chance to prove your suitability for the Naval Service. You will not be asked any trick questions. It's a good idea to try and demonstrate your maturity, self-reliance and the ability to mix with others. You'll be asked to talk about topics such as your family and your hobbies at the interview, but you'll also be asked what you've learnt so far about the Service and your Branch of Choice.

You'll be told after the interview whether you may progress to Stage 4.

Stage 4

It is necessary for you to pass a medical examination, so you can be considered fit for active service.

All successful candidates need to complete a Security Questionnaire. Security vetting includes a check by the security authorities against the National Collection of Criminal Records and a Credit Reference Check.

Once you've successfully completed Stages 1-4, your application will be forwarded to the Ministry of Defence, which needs to approve all candidates' applications. After a decision has been made you'll receive a letter telling you if you have been selected.

The Admiralty Interview Board

All applicants for a commission in the Royal Navy, the Royal Marines, QARNNS or the Naval Reserve Forces have to successfully pass through the Admiralty Interview Board (AIB).

The purpose of the Board is to assess your potential to become a satisfactory Officer after training. Your success at the AIB will depend upon how you express your personality and character during your time there. In addition you should also be prepared to show your Naval and general knowledge and talk about examples of situations where you've had to demonstrate your initiative.

The AIB is housed in the Wardroom area of HMS *Sultan*. A Board is made up of four members. The first three are Service Officers. The fourth member is an Education Officer, who will be a head teacher from one of a wide range of schools throughout the UK.

In addition to looking for intelligence and the ability to tackle the intellectual demands of training, your assessors will watch to see how you cope with the various challenges you'll face during your stay at the AIB. This, in combination with the academic results you have achieved and your performance in intelligence tests, contributes to the Board being able to assess whether you have the appropriate qualities. You'll also need to prove you have potential in the following:

- drive and energy
- using your intelligence effectively
- expressing yourself clearly
- your motivation to join the Navy
- being able to get on with people
- leadership qualities
- a sense of humour.

The AIB lasts for two and a half days and you'll be put into a mixed group of candidates. Remember that you're being assessed by comparison with well-established standards at the AIB, and not being assessed by direct comparison within your group.

Contact your nearest Armed Forces Careers Office for a copy of the booklet 'Admiralty Interview Board, A Guide for Candidates', which will give you full details of how to prepare and what to expect from the AIB.

JOBS AND OPPORTUNITIES

Once you've made the decision to join the Royal Navy your next choice is choosing your specialisation.

There are many skilled workers in the Royal Navy, from communications specialists to people who supply food and clothing, as well as cooks, medical assistants and those who work with weapons or maintain the aircraft.

The Royal Navy is divided into six branches:

- Warfare
- Engineering
- Supply
- Medical
- Fleet Air Arm
- Submarine Service.

WARFARE BRANCH

The Warfare Branch is made up of the people who operate and maintain ship and submarine weapons systems, gathering and co-ordinating information and helping to guide the weapons to their targets. They do this under the direction of Weapons Engineering Branch Technicians, known as Artificers in the Royal Navy.

Jobs:

Abovewater Warfare
Underwater Warfare

Mine Warfare
Electronic Warfare
Communications
Communications Technician
Survey Recorder
Submarine Warfare
Sensors Submarine
Weapons Submarine
Communications Submarine
Tactical Submarine.

ENGINEERING BRANCH

Technicians and highly trained mechanics keep things running smoothly, including the weapons systems, the aircraft, as well as the ship or submarine itself.

Jobs:

Engineering Technician (Artificer)
Air Engineering Mechanic
Marine Engineering Mechanic.

SUPPLY BRANCH

These are the people who have to think of everything months in advance, from planning menus for the next year to knowing where every spare part is.

Jobs:

Chef
Steward
Writer
Stores Accountant.

MEDICAL BRANCH

These are professionals trained in a wide range of medical skills, caring for the sick and injured with the full back-up of the Naval Hospital service.

Jobs:

General Service Medical Assistant
The Commando Medical Assistant
The Submarine Medical Assistant (men only)
The Medical Assistant – Operating Department Practitioner
Registered Nurse (Mental Health)
Dental Surgery Assistant
Leading Dental Hygienist.

FLEET AIR ARM

The Fleet Air Arm provides the aircraft – helicopters and fixed wing aircraft, operated by pilots and observers and supported by naval airmen – aircraft handlers, survival equipment specialists, meteorologists and oceanographers.

Jobs:

Naval Airman (Aircraft Handling)
Naval Airman (Survival Equipment)
Naval Airman (Meteorology and Oceanography).

SUBMARINE SERVICE

Submarines are the UK's front-line, 24-hour protection force, cruising the world beneath the ocean surface, sometimes for as long as three months at a time. As a Submariner you'll be paid more than a surface ship sailor. The atmosphere aboard a submarine is much more relaxed than it is aboard most surface ships. And the men who run the submarines often stay in this branch throughout their Navy careers because they like the life. At present women are not eligible to join the Submarine Service.

Jobs:

Sensors Submariner
Weapons Submariner
Tactical Submariner
Communications Submariner
Marine Engineering Artificer
Weapon Engineering Artificer
Marine Engineering Mechanic
Chef
Steward
Stores Accountant
Writer
Medical Assistant.

TRAINING

RECRUIT TRAINING – YOUR FIRST WEEK

You'll start your training at HMS *Raleigh*, near Plymouth, where all Naval Ratings begin their Naval career. You'll go straight to the New Entry Division to meet your Divisional Officer, who will issue you with an enrolment form. If you change your mind at this stage it's no problem to leave. You're not officially in the Navy until after you've signed the enrolment.

During your first week you'll spend time getting used to Navy life and even beginning to understand all the new terms. At first it will seem rather strange but you'll soon feel at home. You will be given your kit when you join and told how to keep it clean and smart, which is very important. You'll begin to gain confidence and get used to a new and exciting life.

THE NEXT SEVEN WEEKS

After your first week you'll move from the New Entry Division to one of the Part 1 Training Divisions and this is where you'll really start working hard. At this stage the Navy is mainly training you to look, think and behave like a sailor getting into the appropriate state of mind. You'll start your trade training later.

You'll undergo lots of practical training, too, including learning how to handle small boats efficiently and safely, as well as being trained in how to fight floods and fires.

Physical education

Physical fitness is very important and you'll spend time on physical education, on the parade ground, in the gym, on the assault course, as well as a weekend adventure training trek on Dartmoor. You'll also be given parade training. Drill is important as it teaches you to work in a team and quickens your responses. You'll also learn how to fire and maintain a self-loading rifle.

Keeping smart

Your ongoing training and the lessons you learnt in the first week about the importance of keeping your kit clean and tidy will be reinforced. This is important as once you're on board ship, with a lot of people living in a confined space, you'll need to look after all your belongings carefully.

Classroom teaching

As well as practical exercises you'll spend some time in the classroom learning about the Navy's history, in addition to periods discussing current affairs and other Naval subjects.

During your third week you'll have an interview with the Personnel Selection Officer just to check on your progress and to ensure you made the right choice of trade when you applied or would be better suited to something else within the Navy.

Time off

It's not all work and no play and you will get some time off when at HMS *Raleigh*. After you've finished the day's training, prepared your kit for the following day, and passed a kit inspection, you may want to take part in one of a large number of sports. Once you've been at *Raleigh* for six weeks you'll be allowed 'shore' leave for a weekend afternoon in either Plymouth or other local places – all subject to a satisfactory kit inspection beforehand!

Passing-out Parade

Your Passing-out Parade will take place at the end of your eight weeks at HMS *Raleigh* and your parents will be invited. You will have come a long way in a relatively short period of time – you'll be fitter and more confident and you'll have worked harder than at any other time in your life. You'll know what it feels like to be an integral part of a team and you will have learnt some useful skills and know there are many more to come.

TRADE TRAINING

After your recruit training comes your trade training. The majority of trades are taught at shore establishments in and around Portsmouth, but sometimes you may stay at HMS *Raleigh* for further training. So, when will you go to sea? Well, some people are trained and at sea within six months of joining the Navy. Others will do a shore-based job after training for up to three years before joining their first ship.

It takes time to learn a trade in the Navy, but for good reason. In a modern ship you'll be handling some complex and very sophisticated equipment and it's essential you know how to operate it, and have some idea of how it works. This takes time and can mean hard study, including some written examinations as well as practical tests.

When you're at sea everyone knows what's expected of them and how to carry it out immediately and smoothly. And, of course, your learning and training will be ongoing. Each new experience and each new challenge will add to your expertise and sharpen your skills. They will all help you to react promptly and correctly to any problem that comes your way.

OFFICER TRAINING

Initial general training

If you pass the Admiralty Interview Board you'll go to Britannia Royal Naval College, Dartmouth, to commence your training, where you'll be taught the skills required to become an officer. The length of your training here is dependent on your qualifications. There are five divisions, each run by its own Divisional Officer, and you will join one of them.

Right from the start you'll be challenged – getting up early to begin work and finishing late, especially during the first few weeks. Your training schedule will include subjects such as basic naval science and engineering, navigation, rigging and ship's organisation, parade training, boatwork, which involves learning seamanship and finding out how to handle a variety of college crafts on the River Dart and around the local coast.

Developing your leadership skills is of paramount importance. This includes a number of practical leadership tasks, including exercises on Dartmoor. On completion of each task you'll look at what you've achieved, and how successful you've been, both individually and as a team.

You'll have the experience of leading a small team during a practical exercise on Dartmoor. This will involve you in a variety of both physically arduous as well as mentally challenging activities. You'll be told the objective of the exercise, but it will be up to you to decide how to get there. You might be faced with the prospect, for example, of being asked to get your team to a rendezvous point several miles away. Do you take the most direct but difficult route across river and bog? Or do you take a longer and easier route? It's your decision, and it's at times like these that your teammates will be looking to you for inspiration.

Specialist training

In your second term you'll commence Initial Sea Training in an operational warship. Eventually, your training will be a longer period at sea, in anything from a single role minehunter to an aircraft carrier or submarine. You will be required to take your Fleet Board examination and you could spend up to nine months studying for this.

On completion of your general training you'll attend relevant courses to your Branch. For example, if you're an Engineer Officer, you'll need to complete a Systems Engineering and Management Course. If you're a Pilot, you'll commence your flying lessons while at the same time studying the theory of flight, meteorology and navigation.

CAREER PATHS

One in four serving Naval Officers began their Navy careers as an Ordinary Rating, so it's up to you to prove you can go all the way up the promotion ladder, if you want to and accept the challenge. Your first step is to progress through the rates, although if you wish it's possible to apply for Officer selection fairly early on.

The ranks and ratings of the Royal Navy are:

Able Rate
Leading Rate
If you work hard to prove you have the kind of aptitude the Navy is seeking, then you have every chance of successfully making it to this rate between the ages of 22 and 23.
Petty Officer
If you're prepared to take on and relish increasing responsibility you could reach the rank of Petty Officer between the ages of 26 and 28.
Chief Petty Officer
By the time you're in your mid-30s, if you're right for the job you'll have the opportunity of promotion to the rank of Chief Petty Officer, if you are recommended and are successful at selection.
Warrant Officer
Promotion to this rank is by selection on the basis of your qualifications and service record. It would be usual in this rank for you to serve at least to the age of 50.
Sub-Lieutenant
Lieutenant
Lieutenant Commander
Commander
Captain.

SALARIES

Pay

Naval pay compares well with most jobs in civilian life. As well as your basic pay, there s additional money for special skills, special service (in submarines for example), good conduct and other qualifications. And if you have to find your own accommodation you ll receive extra money. Salaries are reviewed every year. Contact your Armed Forces Careers Office for up-to-date salaries.

Bonuses and allowances

Ratings entering the Navy on an Open Engagement receive a bonus in the region of £3000 after completing $4^1/2$ years' service and a further bonus of approximately £2500 after $7^1/2$ years' service. A Longer Service at Sea bonus is payable to ratings serving at sea.

Royal Navy Ratings' rates of pay

(Check with your Armed Forces Careers Office for current rates of pay)

Royal Navy—non-Technicians

On entry	£10,344
Able Rating	£12,070–£22,100
Leading Rating	£19,812–£25,342
Petty Officer	£22,926–£28,200
Chief Petty Officer	£25,298–£32,744
Warrant Officer	£29,182–£35,420

Technicians (Artificers and Medical Technicians)

1st year Under Training	£10,727
2nd year Under Training	£12,071
3rd year Under Training	£12,782
4th year Under Training	£18,389

Queen Alexandra's Royal Naval Nursing Service

Student and Qualified Nurses on joining	£10,344

Student and Qualified Nurses after 8 weeks'
 basic training   £12,070
Qualified Nurses on promotion
 (approx. 16 weeks)   £19,812–£25,342

PROFILES

CASE STUDY

James Griggs, Air Engineering Mechanic

James decided he wanted to join the Navy whilst he was in the Sea Cadets. Although he is now only 19, he has been in the Navy for nearly four years.

'After HMS Raleigh I did my basic Qualifying Course at HMS Daedalus at Lee-on-the-Solent. First of all I learnt the basics – how aircraft and helicopters fly, and how to work around aircraft safely and efficiently.

'I next went to Portland Royal Naval Air Station. As well as classroom work I was sent on two-week trips; I visited Madeira, Gibraltar and the Port of Lisbon. The trips were hard work, but worthwhile. You do a week at sea, a couple of days alongside in port and a week travelling back to England.

'Being an Air Engineering Mechanic means I have the best of both worlds. I don't spend all my time in the ship, but I do have the chance of going to sea to do exercises.

'I've just taken an exam for the next higher rate – to become a Leading Hand. If you want to get on, you've got to study. You've got to show motivation.

'I've learnt a lot about engineering and how systems work on aircraft I've also learnt about myself and I think I've grown up an awful lot.

'The Navy is hard work and it is a commitment as well. It's not a nine-to-five job. Yesterday I was up at 8am and worked till 2 o'clock in the morning, but today's schedule is much easier and I'll be finishing much earlier. If you want to join the Navy, and you are sure it's what you want – do it. Otherwise you'll regret it later in life and say "Why didn't I join the Navy?"'

Donna Turnbull, Operator Mechanic (Communications)

Donna is 19 and has been in the Navy for two and a half years – one reason she considered joining is because her father was also in the Navy.

'I was very nervous when I went to train at HMS Raleigh, but so were all the other girls. We went through a lot together, we had to cope with assault courses as well as exams, so we got to know each other really well. At first it nearly killed us! But by the end of the six weeks we got used to it. At times I felt as though I wanted to give up, but I knew I had to go on.

'I have been in HMS Coventry for just over a year now. It is very different from being on shore, because at the end of the day on land you can go away from the job and forget about it. Here you are with it all the time. You get to know not only those in your department who you work with, but almost everybody in the ship.

'On the Bridge I listen to messages as they come through from other ships, shore bases or whoever is transmitting.

'When there are exercises going on I receive a great deal of radio communications in a short space of time. I have to sort out the relevant information and quickly pass it to the Officer of the Watch, and make sure key people get exactly the right information – it can get quite hectic.

'I enjoy being in the Navy, and I think it is good that there are now more opportunities for women. It has taught me to be patient and wait for things to work themselves out. It is like every job – there are good times and bad. But there is nothing else I could have done that would have taught me so much in just a couple of years.'

Lieutenant Matt Moules, Submarine Navigating Officer

Matt joined the Royal Navy from university at the age of 22. In common with all Warfare officers he spent the first two years both ashore and at sea undergoing initial Naval training and learning the skills required to become an officer of the watch.

'I volunteered for the Submarine Service because it offered much more excitement and challenge and I wanted to be part of a professional elite. I was also attracted because it's a little unconventional and, of course, you get paid extra.

'I did my basic training at the Submarine School and then spent seven weeks learning about nuclear physics and reactor operations. This is a fairly demanding course but you don't have to have a degree in nuclear physics to get through it. After an introductory course in submarine warfare I went to sea for a year and got my Dolphins in HMS Triumph before going back to the Submarine School for navigation training and further warfare training.

'After less than four years in the Navy I became the Navigating Officer of HMS Turbulent, responsible for planning the submarine's passage and navigating her into and out of numerous ports. One of the most challenging, but also rewarding, things I've ever done was a night entry into Plymouth after returning from an operational patrol. I hadn't even been out in the fresh air for two and a half months but we got alongside safely and all went ashore for a long-awaited beer!

'As for the future, I've started the Submarine Advanced Warfare Course, which will train me to be a dive officer of the watch. I also hope to do the Specialist Navigator Course, which will open up a host of other jobs, even the possibility of navigating an aircraft carrier. My main ambition, though, is to get my own command. Ultimately I'd like to command a submarine, but there are opportunities even at my level to be the Captain of a small ship.'

THE ROYAL MARINES

The Royal Marines are the Navy's Commandos and offer one of the most challenging, varied and exciting careers.

Open engagement (Royal Navy and Royal Marines entrants)

Recruits can join the Royal Marines for 22 years' pensionable service from the age of 18, or your date of entry, whichever is later.

ENTRY REQUIREMENTS

(Please see the section on Entry Requirements for the Royal Navy on pages 41–43, which is also applicable to the Royal Marines.)

Physical fitness

You will require a high level of physical fitness before joining the Royal Marines. You'll find recruit training is physically demanding and you are best to prepare for this before you come to the Potential Royal Marines Course (PRMC). You should aim to have good all-round fitness when you arrive for your PRMC. This means being able to run comfortably and have enough upper-body strength to be able to lift your own body weight. Unless you've achieved this level of fitness you won't be able to complete the tests to a satisfactory standard.

As a Royal Marines Commando you'll face some of the most dangerous and challenging situations in very hostile environments, so the physical part of your training is absolutely core. However, in addition, the Royal Marines need to assess your intelligence, character and outlook. Your training will turn you into an effective team member, but it's important you have the right attitude from the beginning.

PERSONAL QUALITIES

The Royal Marines place great importance on teamwork as it is through effective teamwork that they achieve their best results. You will be encouraged to look after your compatriots and in the Commando tests the clock only stops when the last man in a group crosses the line.

The Green Beret is the distinctive symbol of Commando troops, demonstrating that those who wear it have attended and passed a gruelling and physically demanding test of endurance, by displaying the Commando qualities of courage, determination, unselfishness and cheerfulness in adversity.

You'll need to prove that you have the required qualities and skills for the Royal Marines. These include fitness, commitment, discipline and self-confidence. You will gain and improve on some of these during your training, but it's necessary to show a level of fitness and determination from the start.

THE SELECTION PROCESS

Entry into the Royal Marines is not open to women, except for the Royal Marines Band Service.

MARINE

For Royal Marines General Duties and other non-Technical and Technical Branches, you'll follow specialised Commando Training at Commando Training Centre Royal Marines (CTCRM), Lympstone. Royal Marines receive their specialist training after completion of the Basic Commando Course.

You must pass the selection test, which includes reasoning, literacy, numeracy and mechanical comprehension, an interview, a medical examination and the Potential Royal Marines Course (see below).

At entry you will need to be between the ages of 16 and 27, but including the day of your 28th birthday only.

MUSICIAN (INCLUDING DRUMMER AND BUGLER)

Musicians serve with the Royal Marines Bands, both at sea and ashore. You will receive full military and orchestral dance band training (or trained as a Drummer and Bugler) at the Royal Marines School of Music.

You'll be required to pass a selection test, which includes reasoning, literacy, numeracy and mechanical comprehension, an interview and a medical examination. You will also need to go through an audition, which includes a dental and fitness check, at the Royal Marines School of Music, where you will also sit your musical aptitude test.

At entry you will need to be between the ages of 16 and 27, but including the day of your 28th birthday only.

See also the section on the Royal Marines Band Service on page 71.

THE POTENTIAL ROYAL MARINES COURSE

You will need to be able to cope with the rigours and demands of training in the Royal Marines, and your first step will be to prove yourself on the PRMC. Prior to attending the PRMC you will have seen your Armed Forces Careers Adviser who will have believed you to be suitable for this compulsory stage in the Royal Marines selection process.

The PRMC is conducted at the CTCRM, Lympstone, about 5 miles from Exmouth and 8 miles from Exeter. Over a period of three days you will need to show that you have the following essential qualities:

- determination
- physical fitness
- stamina
- mental ability
- cool-headedness
- ability to rise to a challenge.

Most importantly, the PRMC is a real opportunity for you to see at close quarters what life in the Royal Marines is really like and discover if you have what it takes to be a Royal Marine.

During your three days at the PRMC you will undergo gym tests, a swimming assessment, parade drill, a high obstacle and assault course, an introduction to some of the weapons used by the Royal Marines, memory testing games, interviews, a 3-mile run and a lecture on the 30-week training course.

OFFICER SELECTION

The Royal Marines are considered to be amongst the world's most highly trained and skilled troops so you will need to be a very special kind of person if you want to lead them. It goes almost without saying that you will have to be very physically fit and intelligent – but you will need more.

Most training for Royal Marines Officers is carried out at the Commando Training Centre, Lympstone. But before officer training you will need to undergo a three-day Potential Officers Course (POC) at Lympstone.

To be eligible for a Potential Officers Course you must have the following:

- at least five GCSE grades (or equivalent) and two A-levels
- be at least 17 years of age
- satisfy the necessary medical standards
- possess the qualities required, and be considered a suitable candidate by your School or Graduate Liaison Officer.

The POC lasts for three days and includes:

Day one: Presentation and film, fitness tests, interviews and essay.
Day two: Assault course and Tarzan course, lecture, endurance course, discussion exercise.
Day three: Swimming, lectures and film, final interview.

If you complete the course satisfactorily this does not necessarily mean you'll automatically be able to join the Royal Marines. By completing the Potential Officers Course you will be recommended to appear before the Admiralty Interview Board (AIB). If you are successful at the AIB you'll be admitted to the Royal Marines. The Royal Marines' AIB is the same as the Royal Navy (see pages 45–46).

JOBS AND OPPORTUNITIES

The Royal Marines offers a wide variety of career opportunities and, once you complete your recruit training, you'll be able to choose from approximately 25 specialisations, all offering a wide range of qualifications. However, in the Royal Marines your primary role will always be that of a Commando. You can volunteer for any specialisation on completion of your recruit training, choosing from the following range:

Assault Engineer
Armourer
Chef
Aircrewman
Clerk
Drill Leader
Driver
Electronic Warfare
Heavy Weapons – Anti-Tank
Heavy Weapons – Air Defence
Heavy Weapons – Mortars
Illustrator
Lancing Craft
General Duties
Royal Marines Medical Assistant
Metalsmith
Military Provost
Physical Training
Mountain Leader
Platoon Weapons
Stores Accountant
Signals
Swimmer Canoeist
Telecommunication Technician
Vehicle Mechanic.

TRAINING

TRAINING TO BECOME A ROYAL MARINES COMMANDO

When you complete the Potential Royal Marines Course you've cleared the first hurdle to becoming a Royal Marine. Your next step is to take on 30 weeks of tough and extremely demanding training that will change you from a civilian to a Royal Marines Commando. The course is arduous, both mentally and physically, but you'll be completing it with up to 60 other recruits, all going through the same experiences and feelings as you. This is also the time you'll make lifelong friendships as you learn to support each other.

So, what will you learn ? Well, by the time you've finished training you'll have a range of skills under your belt:

- thinking and acting as a member of a highly professional force
- knowing how to be an effective team member
- reacting quickly to unpredictable situations on exercise in outdoor conditions
- knowing the importance of being smart in presentation and of good bearing
- Being responsible and looking after your reputation as a Royal Marine.

THE RECRUIT TRAINING SYLLABUS

This takes place at the CTCRM where you will have spent your three days on the PRMC course.

Foundation (weeks 1–3)
Each day's training is full, with plenty of movement between the gymnasium, the training block and the Bottom Field. You'll get up at 6am daily, start your training at 7.55am and finish at 4.40pm. But even when you've finished your training for the day there's still plenty of administration, preparation and cleaning to be done before the activities

of the next day. During this time you'll learn how to salute properly, whom to salute and when. You'll learn how to wear uniforms, make your bed in the proper way and how to keep your accommodation and kit clean. To make sure you have mastered these skills you'll have an inspection every morning and the NCOs, being sticklers for detail, may even check behind your ears!

Long weekend leave

Individual skills training (weeks 4–10)
This is when you'll go through an intensive period of acquiring individual skills, including learning how to handle, fire and maintain weapons. You'll also learn about basic fieldcraft and will be issued with your own rifle at the beginning of this training period. This is part of your equipment but not your own property.

Long weekend leave

Advanced skills training (weeks 11–15)
You will carry out a challenging survival exercise, where you'll learn and practise survival techniques including shelter construction, fire-making, cooking and survival navigation. You will also experience what it's like to fly in a military helicopter and even how to escape if it ditches into water!

Long weekend leave

Operations of war training (weeks 16–23)
The primary purpose of this module is to teach you the skills and knowledge you will need in order to act as a rifleman in a commando unit in all operations of war.

Commando course (weeks 24–26)
This part of the training involves your troop moving to RM Poole to carry out amphibious training and a short exercise.

Long weekend leave

Professional training (weeks 27–29)

The final exercise is designed to test all of the field skills you've been taught throughout the last few months. By this stage you'll probably be tired, almost certainly wet and wondering what's going to happen next. This is deliberate and is designed to be similar to conditions you would experience in a war. In so far as it is possible, the final exercise will be carried out implementing the full range of operational assets such as helicopters and boats.

King's Squad (week 30)

The King's Squad Pass Out Day takes place in front of your families and friends. You'll be presented with your Green Beret and having undergone such arduous training you'll realise why those who wear it are held in such high regard worldwide.

Royal Marines officer training

Royal Marines officer training is conducted at Commando Training Centre Royal Marines, Lympstone, over a period of 12 months. The purpose of the training is to give you the skills it takes to become a Royal Marines Officer. Just under half of the training will be in the classroom, and you'll be required to sit exams regularly. In addition, at each stage you'll be involved in carrying out a number of field exercises, lasting from three days to a fortnight, in training areas ranging from Dartmoor to Scotland.

Your officer training will fall into a number of distinct areas.

Initial training

Initial training lasts for nine weeks and this will give you basic training in drill and weapon handling. You'll learn how to look after your equipment and considerable importance will be given to developing your fitness. At this stage you'll learn about Service customs, the role of the Corps, your officer responsibilities, as well as map reading, fieldcraft, first aid and signals.

Military training

During the next 13 weeks of training the physical demands increase and you'll move from gym work to tackling the assault course. Exercises will be true to life and you'll experience what it's like to put practical plans into practice. Your classroom work will include military law and its application, current affairs, information technology, and nuclear biological and chemical defence. You will be taught how to use support weapons and master other techniques such as held engineering and operations in built-up areas.

Amphibious training

You will spend an intensive week at RM Poole being introduced to amphibious warfare. You'll learn about the history of amphibious warfare and look at case studies. Practical training plays an important part and you will have a familiarisation day, putting your skills into practice with the Special Boat Service.

Commando training

This course lasts for four weeks and during that time you will increase your physical training with practical amphibious and patrolling exercises, plus you'll learn more about important survival techniques. At the end of the course you will face Commando Test Week, which includes a 9-mile speed march, the endurance course, the Tarzan assault course, and the '30-miler', all completed with 32lbs of kit on your back. Once you've successfully completed the last test you'll receive the coveted Green Beret.

Advanced military training

As part of this last stage you will learn more about resources and initiative training, a live-firing range package based on instructional and supervision techniques, as well as undergo a ten-day final exercise, which will be the culmination of all your training so far. During this time you will also consolidate your man-management skills, so important as you are appointed to your first troop command after your Pass Out Parade.

CAREER PATHS

You will be able to serve for up to 22 years in the Royal Marines, including training. But how your career develops will depend on numerous factors:

- *What specialisation you have chosen:* Some specialisations are harder to get into than others and have fewer posts for non-commissioned officers and warrant officers.
- *Your education:* In order to be promoted to warrant officer you will need to have the basic educational qualification of two GCSEs at grades A–C (or equivalent), one of which must be English.
- *Your leadership and administrative ability:* Promotion to warrant officer is very selective due to the stringent demands of the jobs that follow.
- *How you have performed on courses:* How well you perform on promotion courses will signify how rapidly you gain promotion and how quickly you can expect to attend subsequent courses.
- *Your annual report:* If you achieve a good series of reports you will increase your chances of promotion.

A typical career path for those joining as a Marine would be: Lance Corporal after 3 years; Corporal after 8 years; Sergeant after 13 years; Colour Sergeant after 16 years.

SALARIES

Contact your Armed Forces Careers Office for current rates of pay and benefits.

Royal Marines	Per annum
On entry	£10,344
Marine	£12,070–£22,100
Corporal	£19,812–£25,342
Sergeant	£22,926–£28,200
Warrant Officer II	£28,218–£33,028
Warrant Officer I	£29,182–£35,420

Other benefits include:

- non-contributory pension on completion of service (22 years)
- 7 weeks' annual paid holiday
- free sport and gymnasium facilities
- subsidised food and accommodation

- free medical and dental care
- discounted rail and coach travel
- a maximum of £175 annual education allowance
- availability of Service married quarters
- advance of pay for buying a house of up to £8500
- removals and relocation package
- civilian accreditation (NVQs) for specialisations
- free rail warrants
- boarding school allowance.

PROFILES

CASE STUDY

Marine Mark Wade

'I was an apprentice with Aston Villa and Hartlepool FC when I left school after which I went on to work for the family business, which involved a lot of office work. Being a keen sportsman who enjoyed an active lifestyle, I knew that working in an office for the rest of my life was not for me. I decided that joining the armed forces was an opportunity for me to achieve the more active lifestyle that I desired. I decided on the Royal Marines because of the sporting activities that range from boxing to bobsleigh, but I also relished the challenge of the rigorous 30 weeks' Commando training.

'Training was very hard and challenging. The first couple of weeks I found the worst because of the massive transition between the civilian and military way of life. After that it started to get easier, as I became more competent with my administration and the training became more enjoyable. During training I met some of the best friends I could hope to make because of everything we went through together, and many lifelong friendships were started.

'Do not be under the impression that you have to be super-fit to join the Royal Marines. The majority of people joining are of average physical ability, but the 30 weeks' training programme is designed to build you up gradually to the standard required to become a Royal Marines Commando. All that you need is a big heart and the determination to succeed.

'The day that I passed out of training, which is known as The King's Squad, was a day that I will never forget. I have never felt so proud or seen my mother and father looking so proud of anything that I have achieved before in my life. It was an amazing day, which will live in my memory forever.

'When I passed out of training I was put on to a Combat Signals Course to become a Signaller. This involved using a range of different radios for communicating on the battlefield.

It is one of the most important jobs for a Marine in the Corps, because of the information that needs to be passed between the Commanding Officer and the men on the ground.

'In the Marines you will get to travel all over the world, from winter deployments in Norway to jungle training in Belize. Life in the Royal Marines will give you confidence and a huge amount of self-belief because you will have been pushed really hard both physically and mentally, and survived'

Marine Philip Hill

'I was born and raised in Zimbabwe and although from a farming background had met a number of ex-Royal Marines over the years. Early in 1997 I was lucky enough to watch X-Company 45 Commando on exercise near my home and having spoken to some of the men decided to join the Corps.

'Early in 1998 I arrived in rainy England from my home in Zimbabwe. I found life in the UK a culture shock to begin with, but nothing compared to the challenges of Royal Marines training. The challenges and the goals seemed endless, and as one was reached another presented itself, but no one ever said it was going to be easy. Life was certainly not dull or slow.

'I completed my 30 weeks' basic and Commando training feeling that I had achieved something special and the course had confirmed that the old boys back in Zimbabwe were certainly right about the challenges. I was sent to 45 Commando for my first draft, which was my preference, and was even more surprised when I joined X-Company, the very people I had seen on exercise over a year before. I went to Norway and America on many exercises with the Company, which I found to be an amazing and excellent experience. After a while I decided I would like to specialise, and having considered many options the one I found most appealing as a Marine was the Assault Engineer (AE) branch. It was a challenging and very enjoyable course, particularly the demolition and counter-mine warfare training. We also trained in basic field construction, improvised bridging, boat handling and water supply. Successful students on completion of the course receive the Basic City & Guilds in Construction Engineering Certificate and with promotion and further advanced AE courses further civilian accredited courses can be taken.

'I have found in nearly three years of service that the lifestyle has all that I had hoped for: fitness, sport, challenges, travel and most importantly top-class mates. I have recently begun preparing for the Junior Command Course that allows me to be considered for further promotion. The Corps was certainly the right choice for me and I have never looked back or regretted joining!'

Corporal John Richards

'After a year working on a Youth Training Scheme in vehicle mechanics I joined the Royal Air Force and went on to serve as an Aircraft Painter and Refinisher. After seven years I decided I needed a challenge but wished to stay within the armed forces. At the age of 25 I transferred Service to the Royal Marines.

'The Royal Marines seemed the ideal choice for what I wanted to go on to achieve at that time in my military career. On successfully transferring Service I joined the Commando Training Centre Royal Marines, where I undertook the longest basic infantry course in the world. It was hard work but the rewards were worth it.

'On completion of training I went on to serve in various units in Scotland, employed as a Rifleman and later a Section Commander. This occupation saw me travelling to and working in places that you would probably never see as a civilian. The last three years have seen me based with 40 Commando in Taunton, Somerset, where I gained promotion.

'Now a Corporal, I am currently attending a Physical Training Instructors Course back at CTCRM. Again another challenging course, but enjoyable. I am at last realising a dream. The Royal Marines in my opinion is an excellent life for any young man. It gives me a sense of pride, belonging and satisfaction, which you'd probably not have in any other team.'

THE ROYAL MARINES RESERVE

The Royal Marines Reserve (RMR) is open to men between the ages of 17 and 30. It provides a force of volunteers acting as a general reserve to the Regular Corps and has approximately 600 trained ranks, of whom roughly 10 per cent are working with the Corps on long-term attachments in all of the regular units.

If you wish to join the RMR you have to pass the same Commando tests at CTCRM in the same times as your regular counterparts. In addition you'll take part in four months of weekend training and one evening a week at your RMR unit before attending a two-week Phase 1 course at CTCRM.

When you've successfully completed Phase 1 training you will have another eight months at your RMR unit before coming back to CTCRM for the two-week Reserve Forces Commando Course.

Those in the RMR ranks have many specialisations open to them. These include becoming landing craft coxswains, drill leaders, weapons instructors, drivers, mortar men, assault engineers, physical training instructors, signallers, chefs and swimmer canoeists. RMR courses are abridged versions of those undertaken by regulars, but RMR members are encouraged to work, exercise and operate with the regular Corps whenever they can.

Information can be obtained on the RMR in your area by contacting the Main Centre at one of the addresses or telephone numbers listed on page 83.

THE ROYAL MARINES BAND SERVICE

To be eligible to join the Royal Marines Band Service you must be between the ages of 16 and 28. If you are interested you should visit your nearest Armed Forces Careers Office for further information.

After you've had an interview and medical you'll attend a musical assessment at a regional careers centre conducted by a team from the Royal Marines School of Music. They will assess you and decide if you should be recommended to be invited to the School for an audition and further interview.

At the School you will have to demonstrate that you have musical aptitude, are bright, flexible, fit, hard working and keen to join the Royal Marines as a musician. If all goes well they will offer you a place as a Junior Musician/Musician 2nd Class, the rank at which everyone, including the Principal Director of Music, starts in the Band Service.

When you join you will attend the Royal Marines School of Music for two years and eight months (one year eight months if you join the Buglers Branch). If your instrument category has no vacancies you'll have the opportunity to learn one or even two new instruments. It is common for many players to be 'double-handed' because of the wide range of music, from orchestral to military, performed by the Band Service.

PREPARATION AND SPONSORSHIP

WHAT CAN I DO TO PREPARE TO JOIN ONE OF THE ARMED FORCES?

All the armed forces want people who participate and they will value it if you're a member of any clubs and societies which have given you the opportunity to develop skills and experience in:

- organising events, expeditions and people
- working as part of a team.

If possible, it's a good idea to join a junior Corps locally or at school, which will give you experience of military life. Even if you've been a cub, brownie, scout or guide, it will all be useful experience.

It's important to be physically fit and healthy to join the armed forces so don't leave it too late – start exercising now!

Find out as much as you can about your chosen Service and about the area of work that interests you most. Read the relevant literature, look at the websites and if possible talk to people who have had some real-life experience of the forces.

But most importantly of all – visit your local Armed Forces Careers Advisory Office. There you'll find out everything you need to know and where to stare. You can find the addresses of all the offices nationwide at the end of this book.

INTERESTED IN FINDING OUT MORE ABOUT THE RAF?

University Air Squadrons

If you're at university, or are going to university, then find out about your University Air Squadron (UAS). Every university has one, which will have full-time RAF staff, including a number of instructors. As undergraduates, members of University Air Squadrons are provided with free flying training. During your first year you'll be expected to do at least 40 hours of ground training during term time. And in addition to summer camps you'll have plenty of opportunity to extend your flying experience at Easter camps or detachments.

If you join a UAS you'll have the experience of being at the controls of a light aircraft, as well as finding out what life is like as an officer in the RAF.

Places are limited and selection is not automatic but if you're interested in finding out more contact your UAS.

INTERESTED IN FINDING OUT MORE ABOUT THE ROYAL NAVY?

A good first step would be to visit your local Armed Forces Careers Office and take a look at the Navy's video about HMS *Raleigh*.

If you want to prepare to apply for the Royal Navy, then getting yourself into good physical shape beforehand will help. When you arrive at HMS *Raleigh* at Torpoint in Cornwall you'll need to be fit, although you'll be considerably fitter by the time you've completed your training. This applies to both men and women. Spending time in your local gym or on the playing fields will certainly help you once you're at HMS *Raleigh*.

It's also a good idea to make sure you can swim before you arrive at HMS *Raleigh*. The Navy will teach you to swim if you can't, but this will be in your own time and will definitely make your time at *Raleigh* more difficult.

Engineering sponsorship

If you're intelligent, highly motivated and display good leadership potential, and are interested in joining the Royal Navy and becoming an Engineer Officer, then you may be eligible for the Engineering Sponsorship Scheme (ESS).

You need to be under 23 and be able to satisfy the academic entry requirements for the University of Southampton, in addition to the minimum education qualifications for officer entry. The ESS sponsors around 40 students every year to read Mechanical Engineering (for future marine engineers) and Electronic Systems Engineering (for air engineers). This Scheme is co-ordinated by the University of Southampton's Royal Naval Support Unit.

As well as your bursary you'll be given payment for attendance at the Support Unit. You will need to do a minimum of 45 Naval training days each year and a selection of maritime/adventure training, as well as deployments during university vacations. During this time you'll begin to understand how the Royal Navy operates, its traditions, and what will be expected of you when you join.

University Cadetship (Royal Navy and Royal Marines)

The University Cadetship is for people who want to get into the Royal Navy or Royal Marines. There are two points of entry, depending on Service requirements:

- You can join on the Royal Navy University Cadetship (Deferred) Entry in September. This allows you to complete one full year of Naval training before beginning your degree course. You will undergo two terms at Britannia Royal Naval College, Dartmouth, including a period of Initial Sea Training, followed by five months' Fleet Training in an operational warship.
- You can join on a Royal Marines University Cadetship. You start in September, and spend a short period at Commando Training Centre, Lympstone, before going straight to university.

You should anticipate graduating before the age of 26 if you wish to join the Navy, or 25 if you wish to join the Royal Marines. You'll be paid a substantial salary during each year of study.

But if you're not successful in gaining a scholarship, bursary or University Cadetship you can still join the Royal Navy or Royal Marines through the normal Naval College Entry as long as you have the required minimum A-level or equivalent qualifications, or after you graduate.

Bursary (Royal Navy and Royal Marines)

A bursary is more flexible if you're not entirely sure that you want to be a Naval officer while reading for your degree. It's open to candidates for the Royal Navy and the Royal Marines and you'll stay a civilian while at university or college, while receiving a tax-free bursary each year.

However, although you stay a civilian while studying, you'll need to spend some of your vacations getting acquainted with the Service you'll be joining.

INTERESTED IN FINDING OUT MORE ABOUT THE ROYAL MARINES?

Start by going to an Armed Forces Careers Office where trained and experienced Careers Advisers will talk to you about yourself and your reasons for wanting to join the Royal Marines.

They'll be able to tell you if you're a suitable candidate and, if you are, they'll let you know what will happen at every stage. If you choose to apply you'll be given a booklet about the selection procedure and an application form to take home. After you've applied you'll return to the Careers Office to sit a written test, have an interview and a medical check.

For information about sponsorship for the Royal Marines, see the above section on the Royal Navy.

INTERESTED IN FINDING OUT MORE ABOUT THE ARMY?

Sponsorship from the Army gives you the added bonus of some financial security whilst you study for your degree, as well as giving you the chance to take advantage of the wealth of opportunities on offer at university and guaranteeing you excellent training at the Royal Military Academy Sandhurst (RMAS) after you graduate.

Army Undergraduate Bursary

An Army Undergraduate Bursary is worth around £6000, based on three years at university with a Bursary throughout.

If you've passed the Regular Commissions Board (RCB) by 1 August or 1 February, the Bursary Board will consider you in September or March. You must make sure you apply for RCB by 31 May or 30 November to meet these deadlines.

The Bursary Conditions are:

- You must serve three years on a Shore Service Commission (SSC) after completing the 44-week Commissioning Course at RMAS (unless you join the Army Air Corps, when you must serve for six years due to the investment in your pilot training).
- You are required to join the University Officer Training Corps (UOTC) and agree with the Commanding Officer on your amount of training. You'll receive payment for any training you carry out with the UOTC at basic Regular Army rates and you'll also receive extra for any holiday attachments.

Who can apply?
You will need to have:

- Applied to the RCB for selection as an Army officer or if you have already passed the RCB.
- A place confirmed for a recognised first degree at a UK university or college of higher education. If your place is conditional you can still apply but the award depends on confirmation of acceptance.
- Agreed to enter RMAS on the first Commissioning Course after you graduate, which is expected to be before your 29th birthday.
- Satisfied the nationality and residency rules.
- Meet the required medical standards.

Postgraduate studies

Most awards are for first-degree courses but if you didn't receive Army sponsorship for your first degree, you may be considered for sponsorship for a second degree.

Veterinary Bursaries

The Army grants bursaries to selected veterinary students who have passed the RCB. This consists of £1000 a year at university and £3000 on arrival at RMAS. A Bursary doesn't guarantee you a place in the Royal Army Veterinary Corps (RAVC) but if a place isn't available within two years of qualification you'll be released from any obligation to join the Army and won't have to pay back the Bursary.

Medical Cadetships

Medical Cadetships are currently worth in the region of £50,000 each (including the last three years' tuition fees). The closing dates for applications are 1 July, 1 September, 1 February and 1 May.

Dental Cadetships

Dental Cadetships are worth in the region of £30,000 each (including the last two years' tuition fees). The closing dates are six months prior to the start of your fourth or fifth year at university.

INTERESTED IN FINDING OUT MORE ABOUT THE ROYAL AIR FORCE?

RAF Sixth Form Scholarship

RAF Sixth Form Scholarships are available for A-level students looking to join the RAF as officers in specific branches. Under this scheme the RAF can provide you with financial support to help you through your upper sixth year.

If you've been awarded an RAF Sixth Form Scholarship and choose to go on to degree level you'll automatically be offered a Bursary. Whilst at university you'll become a member of the University Air Squadron and, after graduation, you'll join the RAF in the branch you originally selected.

RAF Pilot Scholarship

This scheme is designed to help you join the RAF as a pilot after your A-levels. Once you've achieved the appropriate academic qualifications the RAF will send you on a two-week Preparation for Leadership Course in Scotland. On your return you'll join the RAF and begin your initial officer training. Contact your Armed Forces Careers Office for further information.

University Sponsorship

Occasionally it's possible to offer university sponsorship to undergraduates interested in joining particular branches of the RAF. Contact your local Armed Forces Careers Office for up-to-date information.

Medical and Dental Sponsorship

Sponsorship for medical and dental students may be available, either after completing a Sixth Form Scholarship or as a stand-alone award. To be eligible you muse be studying or intend to study for an accredited medical or dental degree at a UK university teaching hospital or affiliated medical school.

WHERE CAN I FIND OUT MORE?

USEFUL WEBSITES

www.army.mod.uk
www.mycamouflage.co.uk
www.raf.mod.uk
www.royal-navy.mod.uk
www.royal-marines.mod.uk

ARMED FORCES CAREERS OFFICES

For current information about career opportunities in the armed forces please contact your nearest Armed Forces Careers Office (AFCO) by visiting, writing or telephoning one of the offices listed below.

ABERDEEN
AFCO
63 Belmont Street
AB10 1JS
01224 639999

BELFAST
AFCO
Palace Barracks
Holywood
BFPO 806
028 9042 7040

BIRMINGHAM
AFCO
46 The Pallasades
B2 4XD
0121 633 4995

BOURNEMOUTH
AFCO
244 Holdenhurst Road
BH8 8AS
01202 311224

BRIGHTON
AFCO
120 Queen's Road
BN1 3WB
01273 325386

BRISTOL
AFCO
4 Colston Avenue
BS1 4TY
01179 260233

CAMBRIDGE
AFCO
82–88 Hills Road
CB2 1LQ
01223 315118

CANTERBURY
AFCO
17 St Peter's Street
CT1 2BQ
01227 457848

CARDIFF
AFCO
8th Floor
South Gate House
Wood Street
CF1 1GR
029 2072 6813

CARLISLE
AFCO
94–96 English Street
CA3 8ND
01228 523958

CHATHAM
AFCO
1 Dock Road
ME4 4JR
01634 842 273

CHELMSFORD
AFCO
1/3 Dorset House
Duke Street
CM1 1HQ
01245 355134

COVENTRY
AFCO
60 Hereford Street
CV1 1LB
024 7622 6513

DARLINGTON
AFCO
148 Northgate
DL1 1QT
01325 461850

DERBY
AFCO
35/36 Castlefields
Main Centre
DE1 2PE
01332 348120

DUNDEE
AFCO
PO Box 81
29/31 Bank Street
DD1 1RW
01382 227198

DUNFERMLINE
AFCO
32/34 Ease Pore
Fife
KY12 7JB
01383 721 843

EDINBURGH
AFCO
67–83 Shandwick Place
EH2 4SN
0131 310 3100/9

EXETER
AFCO
Fountain House
Western Way
EX1 2DQ
01392 274040

GLASGOW
AFCO
Charlotte House
78 Queen Street
G1 3DN
0141 221 9955

GLOUCESTER
AFCO
Britannia Buildings
The Docks
GL1 2EH
01452 521676

GUILDFORD
AFCO
Stamford House
91 Woodbridge Road
GU1 4QE
01483 302304

HULL
AFCO
Norwich House
Saville Street
HU1 3ES
01482 325902

ILFORD
AFCO
180a Cranbrook Road
IG1 4LR
020 8518 5855

INVERNESS
AFCO
3 Bridge Street
IV1 1HG
01463 233668

IPSWICH
AFCO
37 Silent Street
IP1 1TF
01473 254450

LEEDS
10/14 Bond Court
LS1 2JY
0113 245 8195

LEICESTER
AFCO
St Georges House
6 St Georges Way
LE1 1SH
0116 254 3233

LINCOLN
AFCO
Sibthorpe House
350/352 High Street
LN5 7BN
01522 525661

LIVERPOOL
AFCO
Graeme House
Derby Square
L2 7SD
0151 227 1764

LONDON
AFCO
453/454 Strand
WC2R 0RQ
020 7839 4643

LUTON
AFCO
Dunstable House
Dunstable Road
LU1 1EA
01582 721501

MANCHESTER
AFCO
Petersfield House
29 Peter Street
M2 5QL
0161 835 2923

MIDDLESBROUGH
AFCO
67 Borough Road
TS1 3AE
01642 211749

NEWCASTLE-UPON-TYNE
AFCO
New England House
20 Ridley Place
NE1 8JW
0191 232 7048

NORWICH
AFCO
22 Unthank Road
NR2 1AH
01603 620033

NOTTINGHAM
AFCO
70 Milton Street
Victoria Centre
NG1 3QX
01159 419503

OXFORD
AFCO
35 St Giles
OX1 3LJ
01865 553431

PETERBOROUGH
AFCO
23 Hereward Centre
PE1 1TB
01733 568833

PLYMOUTH
AFCO
Mount Wise
Cumberland Road
Devonport
PL1 4JH
01752 501787

PORTSMOUTH
AFCO
Cambridge Road
PO1 2EN
02392 826536

PRESTON
AFCO
83a Fishergate
PR1 2NJ
01772 555675

REDRUTH
AFCO
Oak House
Chapel Street
TR15 2BY
01209 314143

SHEFFIELD
AFCO
Central Building
1a Church Street
S1 2GJ
0114 272 1476

SHREWSBURY
AFCO
2nd Floor
Princess House
The Square
SY1 1JZ
01743 232541

SOUTHAMPTON
AFCO
152 High Street
Below Bar
SO14 2BT
023 8063 0486

ST HELENS
AFCO
63 College Street
Merseyside
WA10 1TN
01744 739527

STOKE-ON-TRENT
AFCO
36/38 Old Hall Street

Hanley
ST1 3ZY
01782 214688

SWANSEA
AFCO
17/19 Castle Street
SA1 1JF
01792 642516

TAUNTON
AFCO
35 East Street
TA1 3LS
01823 354430

WOLVERHAMPTON
AFCO
43a Queens Street
WV1 3BL
01902 420340

WREXHAM
AFCO
21 Rhosddu Road
LL11 1NF
01978 263334

THE ROYAL MARINES RESERVE (RMR)

RMR Bristol
Dorset House
Litfield Place
Bristol
BS8 3NA
0117 973 3523

RMR London
2 Old Jamaica Road
Bermondsey
London
SE16 4AN
020 7237 4331

RMR Tyne
Anzio House
Quayside
Newcastle-upon-Tyne
NE6 1BU
0191224 0550

RMR Merseyside
RNHQ
Merseyside
East Brunswick Dock
Liverpool
L3 4DZ
0151 707 3346

RMR Scotland
37–51 Birkmyre Road
Govan
Glasgow
G51 3JH
0141 445 6020

UNIVERSITY AIR SQUADRONS

There are 16 University Air Squadrons (UAS) spread throughout the UK. If you're interested in finding out more speak to the squadron representatives at your university's Freshers Fair in September or October, or contact the squadron direct (see below for addresses).

UAS: Aberdeen, Dundee and St Andrews
RAF Leuchars
Officer Commanding, Aberdeen, Dundee and St Andrews Universities Air Squadron, RAF Leuchars, St Andrews, Fife KY16 0JX; 01334 839471.
Affiliated universities: University of Aberdeen, University of Abertay (Dundee), University of St Andrews, University of Dundee, Robert Gordon University Aberdeen .

UAS: Birmingham
RAF Cosford
Officer Commanding, University of Birmingham Air Squadron, Park Grange, Somerset Road, Birmingham B15 2RR; 0121 454 2098.
Affiliated universities: Aston University, University of Birmingham, University of Central England in Birmingham, Coventry University, University of Keele, Staffordshire University, University of Warwick, University of Wolverhampton.

UAS: Bristol
RAF Colerne
Officer Commanding, Bristol University Air Squadron, RAF Rudloe
Manor, Hawthorn, Wiltshire SN13 0PQ; 01225 743240.
Affiliated universities: University of Bath, University of Bristol,
University of Exeter, University of Plymouth, University of the West of
England at Bristol.

UAS: Cambridge
Taversham
Officer Commanding, Cambridge University Air Squadron, 2 Chaucer
Road, Cambridge CB2 2ED; 01223 356942/3.
Affiliated universities: University of Cambridge, University of East
Anglia, University of Essex, Anglia Polytechnic University.

UAS: East Lowlands
RAF Leuchars
Officer Commanding, East Lowlands Universities Air Squadron, RAF
Leuchars, St Andrews, Fife KY16 0JX; 01334 839471.
Affiliated universities: University of Edinburgh, Heriot-Watt University,
Napier University Edinburgh, University of Stirling

UAS: East Midlands
RAF Newton near Nottingham
Officer Commanding, East Midlands Universities Air Squadron,
72 Broadgate, Beeston, Nottingham NG9 2FW; 0115 925 4375.
Affiliated universities: De Montfort University Leicester, University of
Leicester, Loughborough University of Technology, University of
Nottingham, Nottingham Trent University.

UAS: Glasgow and Strathclyde
RAF Glasgow
Officer Commanding, Universities of Glasgow and Strathclyde Air
Squadron, 12 Park Circus, Glasgow G3 6AX; 0141 887 1011.
Affiliated universities: University of Glasgow, Glasgow Caledonian
University, Glasgow School of Art, University of Paisley, University of
Strathclyde.

UAS: Liverpool
RAF Woodvale, near Formby
Officer Commanding, Liverpool University Air Squadron, Mulberry
Court, 128 Mount Pleasant, Liverpool L3 5SR; 0151 709 1124.
Affiliated universities: University of Central Lancashire Preston,
University of Lancaster, University of Liverpool, Liverpool John Moores
University.

UAS: London
RAF Benson near Oxford
Officer Commanding, University of London Air Squadron,
206 Brompton Road, London SW3 2BQ; 020 7589 9057.
Affiliated universities: Brunel University, Canterbury Christ Church
College, City University, University of Greenwich, University of
Hertfordshire, University of Kent at Canterbury, Kingston University,
University of London.

UAS: Manchester and Salford
RAF Woodvale near Formby
Officer Commanding, Manchester and Salford Universities Air
Squadron, RAF Woodvale, Formby, Merseyside L37 7AD; 01704 872287
Affiliated universities: University of Manchester, University of
Manchester Institute of Science and Technology (UMIST), Manchester
Metropolitan University, University of Salford.

UAS: Northumberland
RAF Leeming, near Northallerton
Officer Commanding, Northumbrian Universities Air Squadron, RAF
Leeming, Northallerton, North Yorkshire DL7 9NG; 01677 423041.
Affiliated universities: University of Durham, University of Newcastle-
upon-Tyne, University of Northumbria at Newcastle, University of
Sunderland, University of Teesside.

UAS: Oxford
RAF Benson near Oxford
Officer Commanding, Oxford University Air Squadron, Falklands
House, Oxpens Road, Oxford OX1 1RX: 01865 244634.
Affiliated universities: Cranfield University (OUAS recruits RAFVR
members from the Shrivenham campus only of Cranfield University),

University of Oxford, Oxford Brookes University, University of Reading.

UAS: Royal Military College
The RMCAS is located at the Shrivenham campus of Cranfield University. It has no airfield and its members are those RAF-sponsored students studying at the Royal Military College of Science.
Officer Commanding, The Royal Military College Air Squadron, Royal Military College of Science, Cranfield University, Shrivenham, Swindon, Wiltshire SN6 8LA.
Affiliated university: Cranfield University.

UAS: Southampton
RAF Boscombe Down
Officer Commanding, Southampton University Air Squadron, 1A Bugle Street, Southampton SO14 2AL; 023 8033 3161/2.
Affiliated universities: University of Portsmouth, University of Southampton.

UAS: Wales
RAF St Athan
Officer Commanding, University of Wales Air Squadron, RAF St Athan, Barry, Vale of Glamorgan CF62 4WA; 01446 797401.
Affiliated universities: University of Glamorgan, University of Wales Aberystwyth, University of Wales Bangor, University of Wales Cardiff, University of Wales College of Medicine, University of Wales Lampeter, University of Wales Swansea.

UAS: Yorkshire
RAF Church Fenton
Officer Commanding, Yorkshire Universities Air Squadron, RAF Church Fenton, Tadcaster, North Yorkshire LS24 9SE; 01347 848261.
Affiliated universities: University of Bradford, University of Huddersfield, University of Hull, University of Humberside Hull, University of Leeds, Leeds Metropolitan University, University of Sheffield, Sheffield Hallam University, University of York.